CALIFORNIA

GO MATH

Middle School
Accelerated Grade 7

Practice and Skills
Fluency Workbook

Contents

Student Worksheets

Name _____ Date _____ Class_____

LESSON
1-1

Adding Integers with the Same Sign
Practice and Problem Solving: A/B

Find each sum. White counters are positive. Black counters are negative.

1. $-5 + (-3)$

   ⬤ ⬤ ⬤ ⬤ ⬤

   ⬤ ⬤ ⬤

   a. How many counters are there? _____

   b. Do the counters represent positive

      or negative integers? _____

   c. $-5 + (-3) =$ _____

2. $-4 + (-7)$

   ⬤ ⬤ ⬤ ⬤

   ⬤ ⬤ ⬤ ⬤ ⬤ ⬤ ⬤

   a. How many counters are there? _____

   b. Do the counters represent positive

      or negative integers? _____

   c. $-4 + (-7) =$ _____

Model each addition problem on the number line to find each sum.

3. $-4 + (-2) =$ _____

   ```
   ←—+—+—+—+—+—+—+—+—→
    -8 -7 -6 -5 -4 -3 -2 -1  0
   ```

4. $-5 + (-5) =$ _____

   ```
   ←—+———+———+———+———+—→
    -20   -16   -12    -8    -4
   ```

5. $-3 + (-6) =$ _____

   ```
   ←—+—+—+—+—+—+—+—+—→
    -11 -10 -9 -8 -7 -6 -5 -4 -3
   ```

6. $-7 + (-5) =$ _____

   ```
   ←—+—+—+—+—+—+—+—+—→
    -13 -12 -11 -10 -9 -8 -7 -6 -5
   ```

Find each sum.

7. $-7 + (-1) =$ _____

8. $-5 + (-4) =$ _____

9. $-36 + (-17) =$ _____

10. $-51 + (-42) =$ _____

11. $98 + 126 =$ _____

12. $-20 + (-75) =$ _____

13. $-350 + (-250) =$ _____

14. $-110 + (-1200) =$ _____

Solve.

15. A construction crew is digging a hole. On the first day, they dug a hole
    3 feet deep. On the second day, they dug 2 more feet. On the third
    day, they dug 4 more feet. Write a sum of negative numbers to
    represent this situation. Find the total sum and explain how it is
    related to the problem.

    _____

LESSON 1-1

Adding Integers with the Same Sign
Reteach

How do you add integers with the same sign?

Add $4 + 5$.	Add $-3 + (-4)$.
Step 1 Check the signs. Are the integers both positive or negative?	**Step 1** Check the signs. Are the integers both positive or negative?
4 and 5 are both positive.	-3 and -4 are both negative.
Step 2 Add the integers.	**Step 2** Ignore the negative signs for now. Add the integers.
$4 + 5 = 9$	$3 + 4 = 7$
Step 3 Write the sum as a positive number.	**Step 3** Write the sum as a negative number.
$4 + 5 = 9$	$-3 + (-4) = -7$

Find each sum.

1. $3 + 6$

   a. Are the integers both positive or

   negative? _____

   b. Add the integers. _____

   c. Write the sum. $3 + 6 =$ _____

2. $-7 + (-1)$

   a. Are the integers both positive or

   negative? _____

   b. Add the integers. _____

   c. Write the sum. $-7 + (-1) =$ _____

3. $-5 + (-2)$

   a. Are the integers both positive or

   negative? _____

   b. Add the integers. _____

   c. Write the sum. $-5 + (-2) =$ _____

4. $6 + 4$

   a. Are the integers both positive or

   negative? _____

   b. Add the integers. _____

   c. Write the sum. $6 + 4 =$ _____

Find each sum.

5. $-10 + (-3) =$ _____

6. $-4 + (-12) =$ _____

7. $22 + 15 =$ _____

8. $-10 + (-31) =$ _____

9. $-18 + (-6) =$ _____

10. $35 + 17 =$ _____

Name _____ Date _____ Class_____

Adding Integers with Different Signs
Practice and Problem Solving: A/B

Show the addition on the number line. Find the sum.

1. $2 + (-3)$ _____

2. $-3 + 4$ _____

Find each sum.

3. $-4 + 9$

4. $7 + (-8)$

5. $-2 + 1$

6. $6 + (-9)$

_____

_____

_____

_____

7. $5 + (-7)$

8. $9 + (-5)$

9. $(-1) + 9$

10. $9 + (-7)$

_____

_____

_____

_____

11. $50 + (-7)$

12. $27 + (-6)$

13. $1 + (-30)$

14. $15 + (-25)$

_____

_____

_____

_____

Solve.

15. The temperature outside dropped 13°F in 7 hours. The final temperature was –2°F. What was the starting temperature?

_____

16. A football team gains 8 yards in one play, then loses 5 yards in the next. What is the team's total yardage for the two plays?

_____

17. Matt is playing a game. He gains 7 points, loses 10 points, gains 2 points, and then loses 8 points. What is his final score?

_____

18. A stock gained 2 points on Monday, lost 5 points on Tuesday, lost 1 point on Wednesday, gained 4 points on Thursday, and lost 6 points on Friday.

   a. Was the net change for the week positive or negative? _____

   b. How much was the gain or loss? _____

Original content Copyright © by Houghton Mifflin Harcourt. Additions and changes to the original content are the responsibility of the instructor.

3

LESSON 1-2

Adding Integers with Different Signs
Reteach

This balance scale "weighs" positive and negative numbers. Negative numbers go on the left of the balance, and positive numbers go on the right.

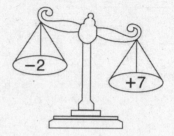

Find −11 + 8.
The scale will tip to the left side because the sum of −11 and +8 is negative.
−11 + 8 = −3

Find −2 + 7.
The scale will tip to the right side because the sum of −2 and +7 is positive.
−2 + 7 = 5

Find 3 + (−9).

1. Should you add or subtract 3 and 9? Why?

   _____

2. Is the sum positive or negative? _____

   $3 + (−9) = −6$

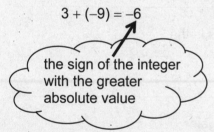

the sign of the integer with the greater absolute value

Find the sum.

3. $7 + (−3) =$ _____

4. $−2 + (−3) =$ _____

5. $−5 + 4 =$ _____

6. $−3 + (−1) =$ _____

7. $−7 + 9 =$ _____

8. $4 + (−9) =$ _____

9. $16 + (−7) =$ _____

10. $−21 + 11 =$ _____

11. $−12 + (−4) =$ _____

12. When adding 3 and −9, how do you know that the sum is negative?

    _____

LESSON
1-3

Subtracting Integers
Practice and Problem Solving: A/B

Show the subtraction on the number line. Find the difference.

1. $-2 - 3$

$-6 \; -5 \; -4 \; -3 \; -2 \; -1 \quad 0 \quad 1 \quad 2$

_____

2. $5 - (-1)$

$-1 \quad 0 \quad 1 \quad 2 \quad 3 \quad 4 \quad 5 \quad 6 \quad 7$

_____

Find the difference.

3. $-6 - 4$

_____

4. $-7 - (-12)$

_____

5. $12 - 16$

_____

6. $5 - (-19)$

_____

7. $-18 - (-18)$

_____

8. $23 - (-23)$

_____

9. $-10 - (-9)$

_____

10. $29 - (-13)$

_____

11. $9 - 15$

_____

12. $-12 - 14$

_____

13. $22 - (-8)$

_____

14. $-16 - (-11)$

_____

Solve.

15. Monday's high temperature was 6°C. The low temperature was –3°C. What was the difference between the high and low temperatures?

_____

16. The temperature in Minneapolis changed from –7°F at 6 A.M. to 7°F at noon. How much did the temperature increase?

_____

17. Friday's high temperature was –1°C. The low temperature was –5°C. What was the difference between the high and low temperatures?

_____

18. The temperature changed from 5°C at 6 P.M. to –2°C at midnight. How much did the temperature decrease?

_____

19. The daytime high temperature on the moon can reach 130°C. The nighttime low temperature can get as low as –110°C. What is the difference between the high and low temperature?

_____

LESSON
1-3
Subtracting Integers
Reteach

The total value of the three cards shown is –6.

$$3 + (-4) + (-5) = -6$$

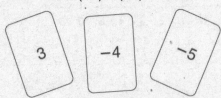

What if you take away the 3 card?

Cards –4 and –5 are left. The new value is –9.

$$-6 + -(3) = -9$$

What if you take away the –4 card?

Cards 3 and –5 are left. The new value is –2.

$$-6 - (-4) = -2$$

Answer each question.

1. Suppose you have the cards shown.
   The total value of the cards is 12.

   a. What if you take away the 7 card? $12 - 7 =$ _____

   b. What if you take away the 13 card? $12 - 13 =$ _____

   c. What if you take away the –8 card? $12 - (-8) =$ _____

2. Subtract –4 – (–2).

   a. $-4 < -2$. Will the answer be positive or negative? _____

   b. $|4| - |2| =$ _____

   c. $-4 - (-2) =$ _____

Find the difference.

3. $31 - (-9) =$ _____   4. $15 - 18 =$ _____   5. $-9 - 17 =$ _____

6. $-8 - (-8) =$ _____   7. $29 - (-2) =$ _____   8. $13 - 18 =$ _____

Applying Addition and Subtraction of Integers

Practice and Problem Solving: A/B

Write an expression to represent the situation. Then solve by finding the value of the expression.

1. Owen is fishing from a dock. He starts with the bait 2 feet below the surface of the water. He reels out the bait 19 feet, then reels it back in 7 feet. What is the final position of the bait relative to the surface of the water?

   _____

2. Rita earned 45 points on a test. She lost 8 points, earned 53 points, then lost 6 more points. What is Rita's final score on the test?

   _____

Find the value of each expression.

3. $-7 + 12 + 15$

   _____

4. $-5 - 9 - 13$

   _____

5. $40 - 33 + 11$

   _____

6. $57 + 63 - 10$

   _____

7. $-21 - 17 + 25 + 65$

   _____

8. $12 + 19 + 5 - 2$

   _____

Compare the expressions. Write <, > or =.

9. $-15 + 3 - 7$ ◯ $-9 - 1 + 16$

10. $31 - 4 + 6$ ◯ $-17 + 22 - 5$

Solve.

11. Anna and Maya are competing in a dance tournament where dance moves are worth a certain number of points. If a dance move is done correctly, the dancer earns points. If a dance move is done incorrectly, the dancer loses points. Anna currently has 225 points.

    a. Before her dance routine ends, Anna earns 75 points and loses 30 points. Write and solve an expression to find Anna's final score.

       _____

    b. Maya's final score is 298. Which dancer has the greater final score?

       _____

LESSON
1-4
Applying Addition and Subtraction of Integers
Reteach

How do you find the value of expressions involving addition and subtraction of integers?

Find the value of $17 - 40 + 5$.

$(17 + 5) - 40$	Regroup the integers with the same sign.
$22 - 40$	Add inside the parentheses.
$22 - 40 = -18$	Subtract.

So, $17 - 40 + 5 = -18$.

Find the value of each expression.

1. $10 - 19 + 5$

   a. Regroup the integers.

   _____

   b. Add and subtract.

   _____

   c. Write the sum. $10 - 19 + 5 =$ _____

2. $-15 + 14 - 3$

   a. Regroup the integers.

   _____

   b. Add and subtract.

   _____

   c. Write the sum. $-15 + 14 - 3 =$ _____

3. $-80 + 10 - 6$

   a. Regroup the integers.

   _____

   b. Add and subtract.

   _____

   c. Write the sum. $-80 + 10 - 6 =$ _____

4. $7 - 21 + 13$

   a. Regroup the integers.

   _____

   b. Add and subtract.

   _____

   c. Write the sum. $7 - 21 + 13 =$ _____

5. $-5 + 13 - 6 + 2$

   a. Regroup the integers.

   _____

   b. Add and subtract.

   _____

   c. Write the sum. $-5 + 13 - 6 + 2 =$ ____

6. $18 - 4 + 6 - 30$

   a. Regroup the integers.

   _____

   b. Add and subtract.

   _____

   c. Write the sum. $18 - 4 + 6 - 30 =$ ____

LESSON 2-1 Multiplying Integers

Practice and Problem Solving: A/B

Find each product.

1. 4(−20)

2. −6(12)

3. (−8)(−5)

_____ _____ _____

4. (13)(−3)

5. (−10)(0)

6. (−5)(16)

_____ _____ _____

7. (−9)(−21)

8. 11(−1)

9. 18(−4)

_____ _____ _____

10. 10(8)

11. 9(−6)

12. −7(−7)

_____ _____ _____

Write a mathematical expression to represent each situation. Then find the value of the expression to solve the problem.

13. You play a game where you score −6 points on the first turn and on each of the next 3 turns. What is your score after those 4 turns?

_____

14. The outdoor temperature declines 3 degrees each hour for 5 hours. What is the change in temperature at the end of those 5 hours?

_____

15. You have $200 in a savings account. Each week for 8 weeks, you take out $18 for spending money. How much money is in your account at the end of 8 weeks?

_____

16. The outdoor temperature was 8 degrees at midnight. The temperature declined 5 degrees during each of the next 3 hours. What was the temperature at 3 A.M.?

_____

17. The price of a stock was $325 a share. The price of the stock went down $25 each week for 6 weeks. What was the price of that stock at the end of 6 weeks?

_____

LESSON 2-1

Multiplying Integers
Reteach

You can use patterns to learn about multiplying integers.

$6(2) = 12$

$6(1) = 6$ -6 Each product is 6 less than the previous product.

$6(0) = 0$ -6 The product of two positive integers is positive.

$6(-1) = -6$ -6 The product of a positive integer and a negative integer is negative.

$6(-2) = -12$ -6

Here is another pattern.

$-6(2) = -12$

$-6(1) = -6$ $+6$ Each product is 6 more than the previous product.

$-6(0) = 0$ $+6$ The product of a negative integer and a positive integer is negative.

$-6(-1) = 6$ $+6$ The product of two negative integers is positive.

$-6(-2) = 12$ $+6$

Find each product.

1. $1(-2)$

   Think: $1 \times 2 = 2$. A negative and a positive integer have a negative product.

2. $-6(-3)$

   Think: $6 \times 3 = 18$. Two negative integers have a positive product.

_____

3. $(5)(-1)$

4. $(-9)(-6)$

5. $11(4)$

_____

Write a mathematical expression to represent each situation. Then find the value of the expression to solve the problem.

6. You are playing a game. You start at 0. Then you score -8 points on each of 4 turns. What is your score after those 4 turns?

_____

7. A mountaineer descends a mountain for 5 hours. On average, she climbs down 500 feet each hour. What is her change in elevation after 5 hours?

_____

LESSON 2-2

Dividing Integers
Practice and Problem Solving: A/B

Find each quotient.

1. $7\overline{)-84}$

2. $-38 \div (-2)$

3. $-27\overline{)81}$

_____   _____   _____

4. $-28 \div 7$

5. $-121 \div (-11)$

6. $-35 \div 4$

_____   _____   _____

Simplify.

7. $(-6 - 4) \div 2$

8. $5(-8) \div 4$

9. $-6(-2) \div 4(-3)$

_____   _____   _____

Write a mathematical expression for each phrase.

10. thirty-two divided by the opposite of 4

_____

11. the quotient of the opposite of 30 and 6, plus the opposite of 8

_____

12. the quotient of 12 and the opposite of 3 plus the product of the opposite of 14 and 4

_____

Solve. Show your work.

13. A high school athletic department bought 40 soccer uniforms at a cost of $3,000. After soccer season, they returned some of the uniforms but only received $40 per uniform. What was the difference between what they paid for each uniform and what they got for each return?

_____

14. A commuter has $245 in his commuter savings account. This account changes by −$15 each week he buys a ticket. In one time period, the account changed by −$240.

   a. For how many weeks did the commuter buy tickets?

   _____

   b. How much must he add to his account if he wants to have 20 weeks worth of tickets in his account?

   _____

LESSON 2-2

Dividing Integers
Reteach

You can use a number line to divide a negative integer by a positive integer.

$$-8 \div 4$$

Step 1 Draw the number line.

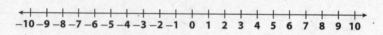

Step 2 Draw an arrow to the left from 0 to the value of the dividend, −8.

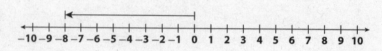

Step 3 Divide the arrow into the same number of small parts as the divisor, 4.

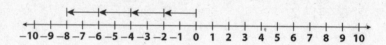

Step 4 How long is each small arrow? When a negative is divided by a positive the quotient is negative, so the sign is negative.

⟵——— Each arrow is −2.

So, $-8 \div 4 = -2$.

On a number line, in which direction will an arrow that represents the dividend point? What is the sign of the divisor? Of the quotient?

1. $54 \div (-9)$

   Dividend: _____

   Sign of
   Divisor: _____

   Sign of
   Quotient: _____

2. $-4\overline{)-52}$

   Dividend: _____

   Sign of
   Divisor: _____

   Sign of
   Quotient: _____

3. $\dfrac{-39}{3}$

   Dividend: _____

   Sign of
   Divisor: _____

   Sign of
   Quotient: _____

Complete the table.

4.

Divisor	Dividend	Quotient
+	+	
	+	
	−	−
		+

LESSON 2-3

Applying Integer Operations
Practice and Problem Solving: A/B

Find the value of each expression.

1. $(-3)(-2) + 8$

2. $(-18) \div 3 + (5)(-2)$

3. $7(-3) - 6$

_____

4. $24 \div (-6)(-2) + 7$

5. $4(-8) + 3$

6. $(-9)(0) + (8)(-5)$

_____

Compare. Write <, =, or >.

7. $(-5)(8) + 3$ ◯ $(-6)(7) + 1$

8. $(-8)(-4) + 16 \div (-4)$ ◯ $(-9)(-3) + 15 \div (-3)$

Write an expression to represent each situation. Then find the value of the expression to solve the problem.

9. Dave owns 15 shares of ABC Mining stock. On Monday, the value of each share rose $2, but on Tuesday the value fell $5. What is the change in the value of Dave's shares?

_____

10. To travel the Erie Canal, a boat must go through locks that raise or lower the boat. Traveling east, a boat would have to be lowered 12 feet at Amsterdam, 11 feet at Tribes Hill, and 8 feet at Randall. By how much does the elevation of the boat change between Amsterdam and Randall?

_____

11. The Gazelle football team made 5 plays in a row where they gained 3 yards on each play. Then they had 2 plays in a row where they lost 12 yards on each play. What is the total change in their position from where they started?

_____

12. On Saturday, Mrs. Armour bought 7 pairs of socks for $3 each, and a sweater for her dog for $12. Then she found a $5 bill on the sidewalk. Over the course of Saturday, what was the change in the amount of money Mrs. Armour had?

_____

LESSON 2-3

Applying Integer Operations
Reteach

To evaluate an expression, follow the order of operations.

1. Multiply and divide in order from left to right.

$$(\mathbf{-5})(\mathbf{6}) + 3 + (-20) \div 4 + 12$$
$$-30 + 3 + (-20) \div 4 + 12$$

$$-30 + 3 + (\mathbf{-20}) \div \mathbf{4} + 12$$
$$-30 + 3 + (-5) + 12$$

2. Add and subtract in order from left to right.

$$\mathbf{-30 + 3} + (-5) + 12$$
$$\mathbf{-27 + (-5)} + 12$$
$$\mathbf{-32 + 12} = -20$$

Name the operation you would do first.

1. $-4 + (3)(-8) + 7$

_____

2. $-3 + (-8) - 6$

_____

3. $16 + 72 \div (-8) + 6(-2)$

_____

4. $17 + 8 + (-16) - 34$

_____

5. $-8 + 13 + (-24) + 6(-4)$

_____

6. $12 \div (-3) + 7(-7)$

_____

7. $(-5)6 + (-12) - 6(9)$

_____

8. $14 - (-9) - 6 - 5$

_____

Find the value of each expression.

9. $(-6) + 5(-2) + 15$

_____

10. $(-8) + (-19) - 4$

_____

11. $3 + 28 \div (-7) + 5(-6)$

_____

12. $15 + 32 + (-8) - 6$

_____

13. $(-5) + 22 + (-7) + 8(-9)$

_____

14. $21 \div (-7) + 5(-9)$

_____

**LESSON
3-1**
Rational Numbers and Decimals
Practice and Problem Solving: A/B

Write each rational number as a terminating decimal.

1. $\dfrac{19}{20}$

2. $-\dfrac{1}{8}$

3. $\dfrac{17}{5}$

_____   _____   _____

Write each rational number as a repeating decimal.

4. $-\dfrac{7}{9}$

5. $\dfrac{11}{15}$

6. $\dfrac{8}{3}$

_____   _____   _____

**Write each mixed number as an improper fraction and as a decimal.
Then tell whether the decimal is terminating or repeating.**

7. $3\dfrac{2}{9}$ _____

8. $15\dfrac{1}{20}$ _____

9. $-5\dfrac{3}{10}$ _____

10. In part a and in part b, use each of the digits 2, 3, and 4 exactly once.

 a. Write a mixed number that has a terminating decimal, and write the decimal.

 _____

 b. Write a mixed number that has a repeating decimal, and write the
 decimal.

 _____

11. The ruler is marked at every $\dfrac{1}{16}$ inch. Do the labeled measurements

 convert to repeating or terminating decimals? _____

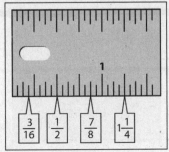

LESSON 3-1

Rational Numbers and Decimals
Reteach

A teacher overheard two students talking about how to write a mixed number as a decimal.

Student 1: I know that $\frac{1}{2}$ is always 0.5, so $6\frac{1}{2}$ is 6.5 and $11\frac{1}{2}$ is 11.5.

I can rewrite any mixed number if the fraction part is $\frac{1}{2}$.

Student 2: You just gave me an idea to separate the whole number part and the fraction part. For $5\frac{1}{3}$, the fraction part is

$\frac{1}{3} = 0.333...$ or $0.\overline{3}$, so $5\frac{1}{3}$ is 5.333... or $5.\overline{3}$.

I can always find a decimal for the fraction part, and then write the decimal next to the whole number part.

The teacher asked the two students to share their ideas with the class.

For each mixed number, find the decimal for the fraction part. Then write the mixed number as a decimal.

1. $7\frac{3}{4}$

_____

2. $11\frac{5}{6}$

_____

3. $12\frac{3}{10}$

_____

4. $8\frac{5}{18}$

_____

For each mixed number, use two methods to write it as a decimal. Do you get the same result using each method?

5. $9\frac{2}{9}$

_____

_____

6. $21\frac{5}{8}$

_____

_____

LESSON 3-2
Adding Rational Numbers
Practice and Problem Solving: A/B

Use a number line to find each sum.

1. $-3 + 4$

2. $1 + (-8)$

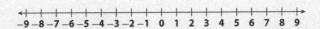

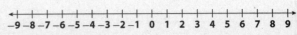

_____   _____

Find each sum without using a number line.

3. $4 + 5$

4. $-3 + \dfrac{1}{2}$

5. $-\dfrac{2}{9} + \dfrac{3}{9}$

_____   _____   _____

6. $-3.5 + (-4.9)$

7. $-2\dfrac{1}{4} + \left(-3\dfrac{1}{4}\right)$

8. $-0.6 + (-2.5)$

_____   _____   _____

9. $-\dfrac{3}{4} + \dfrac{1}{5}$

10. $3 + (-7.5) + 1.2$

11. $-1.32 + 5.02 + (-1.24)$

_____   _____   _____

12. $-3 + (-1.35) + 2.5$

13. $-6.5 + (-0.15) + (-0.2)$

14. $-\dfrac{3}{2} - \dfrac{7}{4} + \dfrac{1}{8}$

_____   _____   _____

Solve.

15. Alex borrowed $12.50 from his friend Danilo. He paid him back $8.75. How much does he still owe?

_____

16. A football team gains 18 yards in one play and then loses 12 yards in the next. What is the team's total yardage?

_____

17. Dee Dee bought an apple for $0.85, a sandwich for $4.50, and a bottle of water for $1.50. How much did Dee Dee spend?

_____

18. Andre went hiking near his house. The first trail he hiked on took him 4.5 miles away from his house. The second trail he hiked took him 2.4 miles closer to his house. The third trail took him 1.7 miles further away from his house. After Andre hiked the three trails, how far from his house was he?

_____

LESSON 3-2

Adding Rational Numbers
Reteach

This balance scale "weighs" positive and negative numbers.
Negative numbers go on the left of the balance. Positive numbers go on the right.

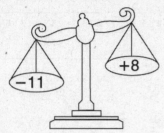 

The scale will tip to the left side because the sum of −11 and + 8 is negative.

The scale will tip to the right side because the sum of $-2\frac{1}{2}$ and + 7 is positive.

Both −0.2 and −1.5 go on the left side. The scale will tip to the left side because the sum of −0.2 and −1.5 is negative.

$$-11 + 8 = -3$$

$$-2\frac{1}{2} + 7 = +4\frac{1}{2}$$

$$-0.2 + (-1.5) = -1.7$$

Find 3 + (−9).

Should you add or subtract?

Will the sum be positive or negative?

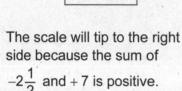

$$3 + (-9) = -6$$

$$|9| - |3|$$

the sign of the integer with the greatest absolute value

Find each sum.

1. −2 + 4 = _____

2. 3 + (−8) = _____

3. −5 + (−2) = _____

4. 2.4 + (−1.8) = _____

5. 1.1 + 3.6 = _____

6. −2.1 + (−3.9) = _____

7. $\frac{4}{5} + \left(-\frac{1}{5}\right) =$ _____

8. $-1\frac{1}{3} + \left(-\frac{1}{3}\right) =$ _____

9. $-\frac{7}{8} + \frac{3}{8} =$ _____

LESSON 3-3

Subtracting Rational Numbers

Practice and Problem Solving: A/B

Use a number line to find each difference.

1. $-5 - 4$

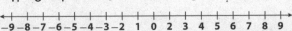

2. $1 - (-8)$

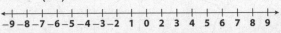

Find each difference without using a number line.

3. $4 - (-5)$

_____

4. $-5 - \dfrac{1}{2}$

_____

5. $\dfrac{1}{7} - \dfrac{3}{7}$

_____

6. $-3.7 - (-4.9)$

_____

7. $-2\dfrac{1}{4} - (-3)$

_____

8. $-1.6 - 2.1$

_____

9. $-4\dfrac{3}{4} - \dfrac{3}{4}$

_____

10. $2 - (-7.5) - 1.2$

_____

11. $-0.02 - 9.02 - 0.04$

_____

12. $4 - (-0.25) - 0.5$

_____

13. $-5.1 - (-0.1) - 1.2$

_____

14. $-\dfrac{3}{5} - \dfrac{7}{5} - \left(-\dfrac{2}{5}\right)$

_____

Solve.

15. The temperature on Monday was $-1.5°C$. The temperature on Tuesday was $2.6°C$ less than the temperature on Monday. What was the temperature on Tuesday?

_____

16. A diver dove to a location $6\dfrac{3}{5}$ meters below sea level. He then dove to a second location $8\dfrac{1}{5}$ meters below sea level. How many meters are there between the two locations?

_____

LESSON
3-3

Subtracting Rational Numbers
Reteach

The total value of the three cards shown is $-4\frac{1}{2}$.

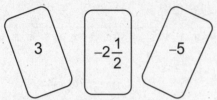

What if you **take away** the $-2\frac{1}{2}$ card?

Cards 3 and -5 are left.
Their sum is -2.

$$\text{So, } -4\frac{1}{2} - \left(-2\frac{1}{2}\right) = -2.$$

What if you **take away** the -5 card?

Cards 3 and $-2\frac{1}{2}$ are left.

Their sum is $\frac{1}{2}$.

$$\text{So, } -4\frac{1}{2} - (-5) = \frac{1}{2}$$

Answer each question.

1. The total value of the three cards shown is 12.

a. What is the value if you take away just the 7? _____

b. What is the value if you take away just the 13? _____

c. What is the value if you take away just the -8? _____

2. Subtract $-4 - (-2)$.

a. $-4 < -2$. So the answer will be a _____ number.

b. $|4| - |2| =$ _____   c. $-4 - (-2) =$ _____

Subtract.

3. $31 - (-9) =$ _____

4. $15 - 18 =$ _____

5. $-9 - 17 =$ _____

6. $2.6 - (-1.6) =$ _____

7. $4.5 - 2.5 =$ _____

8. $-2.0 - 1.25 =$ _____

9. $\frac{4}{5} - \left(-\frac{1}{5}\right) =$ _____

10. $-2\frac{1}{3} - \left(-\frac{1}{3}\right) =$ _____

11. $-\frac{7}{8} - \frac{3}{8} =$ _____

LESSON 3-4

Multiplying Rational Numbers

Practice and Problem Solving: A/B

Use the number line to find each product.

1. $4\left(-\dfrac{1}{2}\right)$ _____

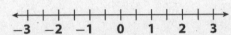

2. $-5\left(-\dfrac{2}{3}\right)$ _____

Find the product.

3. $-2\,(3.1)$

4. $4\,(-5.4)$

5. $-3.3\,(6)$

6. $-3\,(-5.6)$

_____ _____ _____ _____

7. $4.5\,(8)$

8. $2\,(-1.05)$

9. $-2.05\,(4)$

10. $-3.5\,(-9)$

_____ _____ _____ _____

Find the product. Show your work.

11. $\left(\dfrac{2}{3}\right) \times (-6) \times 5 =$ _____

12. $\left(-\dfrac{3}{5}\right)\left(-\dfrac{10}{3}\right)\left(-\dfrac{2}{9}\right) =$ _____

13. $-7 \times \left(-\dfrac{3}{5}\right) \times \left(\dfrac{15}{7}\right) =$ _____

14. $2\,(4)\left(\dfrac{1}{16}\right) =$ _____

Solve. Show your work.

15. A landscaper installs 12 sections of trellis. Each section of trellis is $\dfrac{3}{4}$ yard long. How many yards of trellis are installed altogether?

_____

16. A biologist uses a box-shaped fish trap that measures $\dfrac{1}{4}$-meter by $\dfrac{2}{3}$-meter by $\dfrac{3}{5}$-meter. What is the volume of the trap in cubic meters?

_____

17. The temperature at noon is 75°F. The temperature drops 3 degrees every half hour. What is the temperature at 4 P.M.?

_____

LESSON 3-4

Multiplying Rational Numbers
Reteach

You can use a number line to multiply rational numbers.

$$5 \times \left(-\frac{1}{2}\right)$$

How many times is the $-\frac{1}{2}$ multiplied?

Five times, so there will be 5 jumps of $\frac{1}{2}$ unit each along the number line.

Your first jump begins at 0. In which direction should you move?

$-\frac{1}{2}$ is negative, and 5 is positive. They have different signs. So, each jump will be to the *left*.

(When both numbers have the same sign, each jump will be to the *right*.)

Name the numbers where each jump ends, from the first to the fifth jump.

$$-\frac{1}{2}, \ -1, \ -1\frac{1}{2}, \ -2, \ -2\frac{1}{2}$$

So, $5 \times \left(-\frac{1}{2}\right) = -2\frac{1}{2}$.

Find each product. Draw a number line for help.

1. $6 \times \frac{1}{4}$

   Multiply $\frac{1}{4}$ how many times? _____

   Which direction on the number line? _____

   Move from 0 to where? _____   Product: _____

2. $-8\,(-3.3)$

   Multiply (-3.3) how many times? _____

   Move from 0 to where? _____   Product: _____

3. 4.6×5

   Multiply 4.6 how many times? _____

   Move from 0 to where? _____   Product: _____

LESSON 3-5

Dividing Rational Numbers

Practice and Problem Solving: A/B

Find each quotient.

1. $\dfrac{1}{2} \div (-3)$

2. $-6 \div \left(-\dfrac{3}{4}\right)$

3. $\dfrac{5}{6} \div 10$

_____

4. $\dfrac{5.25}{15}$

5. $24 \div (-3.2)$

6. $-0.125 \div (-0.5)$

_____

7. $-\dfrac{1}{7} \div -\dfrac{3}{14}$

8. $\dfrac{\left(\dfrac{3}{2}\right)}{\left(-\dfrac{9}{8}\right)} =$

9. $-1\dfrac{1}{2} \div 3\dfrac{1}{3}$

_____

10. $2\dfrac{1}{4} \div \dfrac{3}{8}$

11. $\dfrac{4.2}{-2.4}$

12. $-\dfrac{5}{8} \div \left(-\dfrac{5}{16}\right)$

_____

Fill in the blank with a number to make a true statement.

13. $0.25 \div$ _____ $= -0.25$ 14. $-\dfrac{1}{2} \div$ _____ $= -\dfrac{7}{3}$ 15. $\dfrac{1}{7} \div$ _____ $= 14$

Write a division problem for each situation. Then, solve it.

16. How many quarter-pound $\left(\dfrac{1}{4}\right)$ packets of plant food can a garden shop make out of 8 pounds of the plant food?

_____

17. The assembly of a machine takes $\dfrac{3}{4}$ hour. There are 12 steps in the assembly process. What is the average time for each step?

_____

18. A 35-meter length of cable is cut into pieces that measure 1.25 meters each. Into how many pieces is the cable cut?

_____

19. $4\dfrac{1}{8}$ tons of gravel is spread evenly across $2\dfrac{1}{6}$ acres. How many tons of gravel are on each acre?

_____

LESSON 3-5

Dividing Rational Numbers
Reteach

To divide fractions:

- Multiply the first, or "top," number by the reciprocal of the second, or "bottom," number.

- Check the sign.

Divide: $-\dfrac{3}{5} \div \dfrac{2}{3}$

Step 1: Rewrite the problem to multiply by the reciprocal.

$$-\frac{3}{5} \div \frac{2}{3} = -\frac{3}{5} \times \frac{3}{2}$$

Step 2: Multiply.

$$-\frac{3}{5} \times \frac{3}{2} = \frac{-3 \times 3}{5 \times 2} = \frac{-9}{10}$$

Step 3: Check the sign.
A negative divided by a positive is a negative.

So, $\dfrac{-9}{10}$ is correct.

$$-\frac{3}{5} \div \frac{2}{3} = -\frac{9}{10}$$

Write the sign of each quotient. Do not solve the problem.

1. $4\dfrac{1}{4} \div 3\dfrac{1}{2}$

2. $-3.5 \div 0.675$

3. $\dfrac{5}{\left(-\dfrac{3}{5}\right)}$

4. $-\dfrac{2}{9} \div \left(-\dfrac{3}{8}\right)$

_____ _____ _____ _____

Complete the steps described above to find each quotient.

5. $-\dfrac{1}{7} \div \left(-\dfrac{5}{9}\right)$

6. $\dfrac{7}{8} \div \dfrac{8}{9}$

Step 1: _____ Step 1: _____

Step 2: _____ Step 2: _____

Step 3: _____ Step 3: _____

LESSON 3-6

Applying Rational Number Operations

Practice and Problem Solving: A/B

Estimate each answer. Explain your reasoning.

1. Sections of prefabricated fencing are each $4\frac{1}{3}$ feet long. How long are

   $6\frac{1}{2}$ sections placed end to end?

   _____

2. One half liter of lemonade concentrate is added to 3 liters of water.

   How many $\frac{1}{3}$-liter servings of lemonade are made?

   _____

3. Two $2\frac{1}{2}$-inch plastic strips and two $5\frac{1}{3}$-inch plastic strips are used to

   form a rectangle. What is the perimeter of the rectangle?

   _____

4. The average mass of the eggs laid by chickens on Ms. Watson's farm
   is 3.5 grams. About how many grams does a dozen eggs weigh?

   _____

5. An 8.5-centimeter green bean pod contains peas that average
   0.45- centimeter in diameter. How many peas are in the pod?

   _____

**Solve by converting to the easiest form of the rational numbers to use
in the problem. Show your work**

6. Arwen uses a dropper that produces drops that have a volume of

   $\frac{1}{8}$-milliliter to fill a 30-milliliter test tube. How many drops does it take

   to fill the test tube?

   _____

   _____

7. Three strips of 2-yard-wide outdoor carpet are used to cover a sidewalk. One is
   3.5 yards long, the second is 25 percent longer than the first, and the third is

   $6\frac{1}{4}$ yards long. How long are the three carpets placed end to end?

   _____

   _____

Applying Rational Number Operations

LESSON 3-6

Reteach

To multiply fractions and mixed numbers:
Step 1: Write any mixed numbers as improper fractions.
Step 2: Multiply the numerators.
Step 3: Multiply the denominators.
Step 4: Write the answer in simplest form.

Remember, positive times negative equals negative.

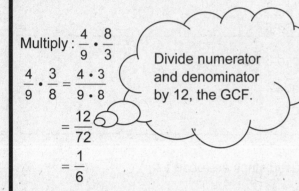

Multiply: $\dfrac{4}{9} \cdot \dfrac{8}{3}$

$\dfrac{4}{9} \cdot \dfrac{3}{8} = \dfrac{4 \cdot 3}{9 \cdot 8}$

Divide numerator and denominator by 12, the GCF.

$= \dfrac{12}{72}$

$= \dfrac{1}{6}$

Multiply: $6\dfrac{1}{4} \cdot \left(-1\dfrac{4}{5}\right)$

$6\dfrac{1}{4} \cdot \left(-1\dfrac{4}{5}\right) = \dfrac{25}{4} \cdot \left(\dfrac{-9}{5}\right)$

$= \dfrac{25 \cdot (-9)}{4 \cdot 5}$

$= \dfrac{-225}{20}$

$= -11\dfrac{1}{4}$

Use the models to solve the problems.

1. One cup of dog food weighs $1\dfrac{4}{5}$ ounces. A police dog eats $6\dfrac{1}{3}$ cups of food a day. How many ounces of food does the dog eat each day?

   _____

2. A painter spends 3 hours working on a painting. A sculptor spends $2\dfrac{2}{3}$ as long working on a sculpture. How long does the sculptor work?

   _____

3. A meteorite found in the United States weighs $\dfrac{7}{10}$ as much as one found in Mongolia. The meteorite found in Mongolia weighs 22 tons. How much does the one found in the United States weigh?

   _____

4. A chicken salad recipe calls for $\dfrac{1}{8}$ pound of chicken per serving. How many pounds of chicken are needed to make $8\dfrac{1}{2}$ servings?

   _____

LESSON 4-1

Unit Rates

Practice and Problem Solving: A/B

Solve.

1. To make 2 batches of nut bars, Jayda needs to use 4 eggs. How many eggs are used in each batch of nut bars?

   _____

2. On her way to visit her parents, Jennifer drives 265 miles in 5 hours. What is her average rate of speed in miles per hour?

   _____

3. Last week Alexander was paid $56 for 7 hours of work. How much money does Alexander's job pay per hour?

   _____

4. Ned has scored 84 points in the first 6 games of the basketball season. How many points per game has Ned scored?

   _____

5. At the local grocery store, a 16-ounce bottle of apple juice costs $3.20. What is the cost of the apple juice per ounce?

   _____

6. An above-ground swimming pool is leaking. After $\frac{1}{2}$ hour the pool has leaked $\frac{7}{8}$ of a gallon of water. How many gallons of water per hour is the swimming pool leaking?

   _____

7. After $\frac{3}{4}$ of a minute a sloth has moved just $\frac{3}{8}$ of a foot. What is the sloth's speed in feet per minute?

   _____

8. Food A contains 150 calories in $\frac{3}{4}$ of a serving. Food B contains 250 calories in $\frac{2}{3}$ of a serving. Find each unit rate. Which food has fewer calories per serving?

   _____

LESSON 4-1

Unit Rates
Reteach

A **rate** is a ratio that compares two *different* kinds of quantities or measurements.

3 aides for 24 students	135 words in 3 minutes	7 ads per 4 pages
$\dfrac{3\ \text{aides}}{24\ \text{students}}$	$\dfrac{135\ \text{words}}{3\ \text{minutes}}$	$\dfrac{7\ \text{ads}}{4\ \text{pages}}$

Express each comparison as a rate in ratio form.

1. 70 students per 2 teachers   2. 3 books in 2 months   3. $52 for 4 hours of work

_____   _____   _____

In a **unit rate**, the quantity in the denominator is 1.

300 miles in 6 hours	275 square feet in 25 minutes
$\dfrac{300\ \text{miles}}{6\ \text{hours}} = \dfrac{300 \div 6}{6 \div 6} = \dfrac{50\ \text{miles}}{1\ \text{hour}}$	$\dfrac{275\ \text{ft}^2}{25\ \text{min}} = \dfrac{275 \div 25}{25 \div 25} = \dfrac{11\ \text{ft}^2}{1\ \text{min}}$

Express each comparison as a unit rate. Show your work.

4. 28 patients for 2 nurses _____

5. 5 quarts for every 2 pounds _____

When one or both of the quantities being compared is a fraction, the rate is expressed as a **complex fraction**. Unit rates can be used to simplify rates containing fractions.

15 miles every $\frac{1}{2}$ hour	$\frac{1}{4}$ cup for every $\frac{2}{3}$ minute
$\dfrac{15\ \text{miles}}{\frac{1}{2}\ \text{hour}} = 15 \div \dfrac{1}{2} = \dfrac{15}{1} \times \dfrac{2}{1} = \dfrac{30\ \text{miles}}{1\ \text{hour}}$	$\dfrac{\frac{1}{4}\ \text{c}}{\frac{2}{3}\ \text{min}} = \dfrac{1}{4} \div \dfrac{2}{3} = \dfrac{1}{4} \times \dfrac{3}{2} = \dfrac{\frac{3}{8}\ \text{c}}{1\ \text{min}}$

Complete to find each unit rate. Show your work.

6. 3 ounces for every $\frac{3}{4}$ cup

7. $3\frac{2}{3}$ feet per $\frac{11}{60}$ hour

_____   _____

Constant Rates of Change
Practice and Problem Solving: A/B

Use the table to determine whether the relationship is proportional. If so, write an equation for the relationship. Tell what each variable you used represents.

1.

Number of tickets	2	3	4	5
Total Cost ($)	54	81	108	135

a. Proportional? _____

b. Equation: _____

c. Number of tickets: _____

d. Total Cost: _____

2.

Weight (lb)	4	5	46
Total Cost ($)	17.40	21.75	200.10

a. Proportional? _____

b. Equation: _____

c. Weight: _____

d. Total cost: _____

3.

Time (h)	2	3	4	5	6
Pages Read	50	75	90	110	120

_____

_____

4.

Time (h)	2	3	4
Distance (mi)	80	120	160

_____

_____

The tables show proportional relationships. Find the constant of proportionality, *k*. Write an equation to represent the relationship between the two quantities. Tell what each variable represents.

5.

Pens	3	6	9	12
Boxes	1	2	3	4

_____

_____

6.

Pack	1	2	4	5
Muffins	6	12	24	30

_____

_____

7. a. Create a table to show how the number of days is related to the number of hours. Show at least 5 days.

  b. Is the relationship proportional? _____

  c. Write an equation for the relationship. _____

Name _____ Date _____ Class_____

 LESSON 4-2

Constant Rates of Change
Reteach

A **proportion** is an equation or statement that two rates are the same.

In 1 hour of babysitting, Rajiv makes $8.
He makes $16 in 2 hours, and $24 in 3 hours.

The same information is shown in the table below.

Time Worked (h)	1	2	3
Total Wage ($)	8	16	24

To see if this relationship is proportional, find out if the rate of change is constant. Express each rate of change shown in the table as a fraction.

$$\frac{8}{1} = 8 \qquad \frac{16}{2} = 8 \qquad \frac{24}{3} = 8$$

The rate of change for each column is the same. Because the rate of change is constant, the relationship is *proportional*.

You can express a proportional relationship by using the equation $y = kx$, where k represents the constant rate of change between x and y.

In this example: $k = 8$. Write the equation as $y = 8x$.

The table shows the number of texts Terri received in certain periods of time.

Time (min)	1	2	3	4
Number of Texts	3	6	9	12

1. Is the relationship between number of texts and time a proportional

   relationship? _____

2. For each column of the table, write a fraction and find k, the constant of proportionality.

   _____

3. Express this relationship in the form of an equation: _____

4. What is the rate of change? _____

Write the equation for each table. Let x be time or weight.

5.

Time (h)	1	2	3	4
Distance (mi)	35	70	105	140

6.

Weight (lb)	3	4	5	6
Cost ($)	21	28	35	42

_____   _____

Name _____ Date _____ Class_____

Proportional Relationships and Graphs

LESSON 4-3

Practice and Problem Solving: A/B

Complete each table. Explain why the relationship is a proportional relationship.

1. A cashier earns $8 per hour.

Time (h)	2	4		
Pay ($)	16		40	72

2. Tomatoes cost $0.70 per pound.

Weight (lb)	2		6	8
Price ($)	1.40	2.10		

_____   _____

_____   _____

Tell whether the relationship is a proportional relationship. Explain your answer.

3.

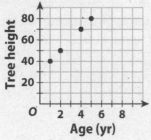

4.

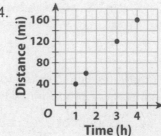

_____   _____

_____   _____

The graph shows the relationship between the distance traveled by a car and the amount of fuel used by the car.

5. Explain the meaning of (2, 40).

_____

_____

6. Write an equation for this relationship.

_____

_____

7. Suppose a compact car uses 1 gallon of fuel for every 27 miles traveled. How would the graph for the compact car compare to the graph for the car shown?

_____

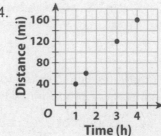

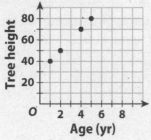

LESSON 4-3
Proportional Relationships and Graphs
Reteach

The graph of a proportional relationship is a line that passes through the origin. An equation of the form $y = kx$ represents a proportional relationship where k is the constant of proportionality.

The graph below shows the relationship between the number of peanut butter sandwiches and the teaspoons of peanut butter used for the sandwiches.

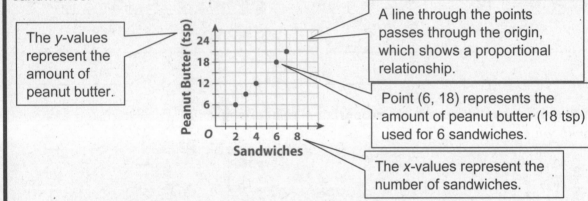

The *y*-values represent the amount of peanut butter.

A line through the points passes through the origin, which shows a proportional relationship.

Point (6, 18) represents the amount of peanut butter (18 tsp) used for 6 sandwiches.

The *x*-values represent the number of sandwiches.

The constant of proportionality k is equal to y divided by x. Use the point (6, 18) to find the constant of proportionality for the relationship above.

$$k = \frac{y}{x} = \frac{\text{amount of peanut butter}}{\text{number of sandwiches}} = \frac{18}{6} = 3$$

Using $k = 3$, an equation for the relationship is $y = 3x$.

Fill in the blanks to write an equation for the given proportional relationship.

1.
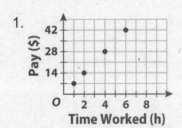

The *x*-values represent _____.

The *y*-values represent _____.

Using point ____, $k = \frac{y}{x} = $ ____ = ____.

An equation for the graph is _____.

2.
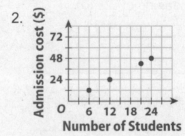

The *x*-values represent _____.

The *y*-values represent _____.

Using point ____, $k = \frac{y}{x} = $ ____ = ____.

An equation for the graph is _____.

LESSON 5-1   Percent Increase and Decrease

Practice and Problem Solving: A/B

Find each percent increase. Round to the nearest percent.

1. From 24 teachers to 30 teachers _____

2. From $18 to $45 _____

3. From 75 pencils to 225 pencils _____

4. From $65 to $144 _____

5. From 42 acres to 72 acres _____

6. From 95 trees to 145 trees _____

Find each percent decrease. Round to the nearest percent.

7. From 20 miles to 11 miles _____

8. From $16 to $4 _____

9. From 126 ounces to 48 ounces _____

10. From 84 seconds to 8 seconds _____

11. From 90 apples to 75 apples _____

12. From 248 workers to 200 workers _____

Given the original amount and the percent of change, find the new amount.

13. $25; 300% increase _____

14. 160 bananas; 20% decrease _____

15. 56 books; 75% decrease _____

16. 52 companies; 25% increase _____

17. 12,000 miles; 5% increase _____

18. 710 points; 10% decrease _____

Solve.

19. Last year, there were 380 students at Woodland Middle School. This year, the student population will increase by 5%. What will be the school's increased student population?

_____

20. A backpack that normally sells for $39 is on sale for 33% off. Find the amount of the discount and the sale price.

_____

21. In August, the Simons' water bill was $48. In September, it was 15% lower. What was the Simons' water bill in September?

_____

22. A gallery owner purchased a very old painting for $3,000. The painting sells at a 325% increase in price. What is the retail price of the painting?

_____

LESSON 5-1 Percent Increase and Decrease
Reteach

A change in a quantity is often described as a percent increase or percent decrease. To calculate a percent increase or decrease, use this equation.

$$\text{percent of change} = \frac{\text{amount of increase or decrease}}{\text{original amount}} \cdot 100$$

Find the percent of change from 28 to 42.

- First, find the amount of the change. $42 - 28 = 14$
- What is the original amount? 28
- Use the equation. $\frac{14}{28} \cdot 100 = 50\%$

An increase from 28 to 42 represents a 50% increase.

Find each percent of change.

1. 8 is increased to 22

   amount of change: 22 – 8 = _____

   original amount: _____

   _____ • 100 = _____%

2. 90 is decreased to 81

   amount of change: 90 – 81 = _____

   original amount: _____

   _____ • 100 = _____%

3. 125 is increased to 200

   amount of change: 200 – 125 = _____

   original amount: _____

   _____ • 100 = _____%

4. 400 is decreased to 60

   amount of change: 400 – 60 = _____

   original amount: _____

   _____ • 100 = _____%

5. 64 is decreased to 48

   _____

6. 140 is increased to 273

   _____

7. 30 is decreased to 6

   _____

8. 15 is increased to 21

   _____

9. 7 is increased to 21

   _____

10. 320 is decreased to 304

   _____

LESSON 5-2

Rewriting Percent Expressions
Practice and Problem Solving: A/B

Use the situation below to complete Exercises 1–6 in the table below.

Discounts R Us buys items at wholesale, then marks them up to set a retail sale price. Some of the items the store sells are shown in the table below.

Item	Wholesale Price	% Markup	$ Markup	Retail Sale Price
1. Notebook	$1.50	20%		
2. Scissors	$3.25	40%		
3. Calculator	$9.60	25%		
4. Sunglasses	$12.50	78%		
5. Bicycle	$78.00	55%		
6. Picture frame	$2.99	150%		

Find the retail sale price of each item below. Round to two decimal places when necessary.

7. Original price: $65.00; Markdown: 12%

8. Original price: $29.99; Markdown: $33\frac{1}{3}$%

_____

9. Original price: $119.00; Markdown: 70%

10. Original price: $325.50; Markdown: 15%

_____

Use the information to complete 11–14.

A jewelry supply shop buys silver chains from a manufacturer for c dollars each, and then sells the chains at a 57% markup.

11. Write the markup as a decimal. _____

12. Write an expression for the retail price of a silver chain.

_____

13. What is the retail price of a silver chain purchased for $45.00?

_____

14. How much was added to the original price of the chain? _____

LESSON 5-2

Rewriting Percent Expressions

Reteach

A **markup** is an example of a percent increase.	A **markdown,** or discount, is an example of a percent decrease.
To calculate a markup, write the markup percentage as a decimal and add 1. Multiply by the original cost.	To calculate a markdown, write the markdown percentage as a decimal and subtract from 1. Multiply by the original price.
A store buys soccer balls from a supplier for $5. The store's markup is 45%. Find the retail price.	A store marks down sweaters by 20%. Find the sale price of a sweater originally priced at $60.
Write the markup as a decimal and add 1.	Write the markup as a decimal and subtract it from 1.
$0.45 + 1 = 1.45$	$1 - 0.2 = 0.8$
Multiply by the original cost.	Multiply by the original cost.
Retail price = $\$5 \times 1.45 = \$7.25$	Sale price = $\$60 \times 0.8 = \$48$

Apply the markup for each item. Then, find the retail price. Round to two decimal places when necessary.

1. Original cost: $45; Markup %: 20%

2. Original cost: $7.50; Markup %: 50%

_____

3. Original cost: $1.25; Markup %: 80%

4. Original cost: $62; Markup %: 35%

_____

Apply the markdown for each item. Then, find the sale price. Round to two decimal places when necessary.

5. Original price: $150; Markdown %: 40%

6. Original price: $18.99; Markdown: 25%

_____

7. Original price: $95; Markdown: 10%

8. Original price: $75; Markdown: 15%

_____

9. A clothing store bought packages of three pairs of socks for $1.75. The store owner marked up the price by 80%.

    a. What is the retail price? _____

    b. After a month, the store owner marks down the retail price by 20%.

       What is the sales price? _____

LESSON 5-3

Applications of Percent
Practice and Problem Solving: A/B

1. Complete the table.

Sale Amount	5% Sales Tax	Total Amount Paid
$67.50		
$98.75		
$399.79		
$1,250.00		
$12,500.00		

2. Complete the table.

Principal	Rate	Time	Interest Earned	New Balance
$300	3%	4 years		
$450		3 years	$67.50	
$500	4.5%		$112.50	
	8%	2 years	$108.00	

Solve.

3. Joanna wants to buy a car. Her parents loan her $5,000 for 5 years at 5% simple interest. How much will Joanna pay in interest?

_____

4. This month Salesperson A made 11% of $67,530. Salesperson B made 8% of $85,740. Who made more commission this month? How much did that salesperson make?

_____

5. Jon earned $38,000 last year. He paid $6,840 for entertainment. What percent of his earnings did Jon pay in entertainment expenses?

_____

6. Nora makes $3,000 a month. The circle graph shows how she spends her money. How much money does Nora spend on each category?

a. rent _____

b. food _____

c. medical _____

d. clothes_____

e. miscellaneous _____

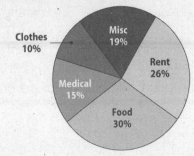

Name _____ Date _____ Class_____

LESSON 5-3

Applications of Percent
Reteach

For any problem involving percent, you can use a simple formula to calculate the percent.

$$amount = percent \times total$$

The amount will be the amount of tax, tip, discount, or whatever you are calculating. Use the formula that has your unknown information before the equal sign.

For simple-interest problems, time is one factor.
So, you must also include time in your formula.

$$amount\ (interest) = total\ (principal) \times percent\ (rate) \times time$$

A. Find the sale price after the discount.

Regular price = $899

Discount rate = 20%

You know the total and the percentage. You don't know the discount amount. Your formula is:

amount = % × total

$$= 0.20 \times \$899$$
$$= \$179.80$$

The amount of discount is $179.80.
The sale price is the original price minus the discount.

$899 − $179.80 = $719.20

The sale price is $719.20

B. A bank offers simple interest on a certificate of deposit. Jamie invests $500 and after one year earns $40 in interest. What was the interest rate on his deposit?

You know the total deposited—the principal. You know the amount earned in interest. You don't know the percentage rate of interest. Since the time is 1 year, your formula is:

% = amount ÷ total
$$= \$40 \div \$500$$
$$= 0.08$$
$$= 8\%$$

The interest rate is 8%.

Johanna purchases a book for $14.95. There is a sales tax of 6.5%. How much is the final price with tax?

1. What is the total in this problem? _____

2. What is the percent? _____

3. Use the formula *amount* = total × percent to find the amount of the sales tax.

   _____

4. To find the final price, add the cost of the book to the amount of tax.

   _____

LESSON 6-1

Algebraic Expressions

Practice and Problem Solving: A/B

Write an algebraic expression for each phrase.

1. Four more than the price, p

2. Five less than three times the length, L

_____   _____

Write a word phrase for each algebraic expression.

3. $25 - 0.6x$

_____

4. $\frac{2}{3}y + 4$

_____

Simplify each expression.

5. $(100 + 4z)20$

6. $0.75(3.5a - 6b)$

_____   _____

Factor each expression.

7. $45c + 10d$

8. $27 - 9x + 15y$

_____   _____

Solve. Show each step.

9. A construction worker bought several bottles of juice for $3 at the convenience store. She paid for them with a $20 bill. If j represents the number of bottles of juice, write an expression for the change she should receive.

_____

10. A giant bamboo plant grew an average of 18 centimeters per year. The botanist started measuring the plant when it was 5 centimeters tall. If y represents the number of years the botanist has measured the plant, what expression represents its height?

_____

Name _____ Date _____ Class _____

Algebraic Expressions
Reteach

LESSON 6-1

Algebraic expressions can be written from verbal descriptions. Likewise, verbal descriptions can be written from algebraic expressions. In both cases, it is important to look for word and number clues.

Algebra from words
"One third of the participants increased by 25."

Clues
Look for "number words," like
- "One third."
- "Of" means multiplied by.
- "Increased by" means add to.

Combine the clues to produce the expression.
- "One third of the participants." $\frac{1}{3}p$ or $\frac{p}{3}$.
- "Increased by 25." +25

"One third of the participants increased by 25."
$\frac{1}{3}p + 25$ or $\frac{p}{3} + 25$

Words from algebra
"Write $0.75n - \frac{1}{2}m$ with words."

Clues
Identify the number of parts of the problem.
- "$0.75n$" means "three fourths of n" or 75 hundredths of n. The exact meaning will depend on the problem.
- "$-$" means "minus," "decreased by," "less than," etc., depending on the context.
- "$\frac{1}{2}m$" is "one half of m" or "m over 2."

Combine the clues to produce a description. "75 hundredths of the population minus half the men."

Write a verbal description for each algebraic expression.

1. $100 - 5n$

2. $0.25r + 0.6s$

3. $\frac{3m - 8n}{13}$

_____

_____

_____

_____

_____

_____

Write an algebraic expression for each verbal description.

4. Half of the seventh graders and one third of the eighth graders were divided into ten teams.

_____

5. Thirty percent of the green house flowers are added to 25 ferns for the school garden.

_____

6. Four less than three times the number of egg orders and six more than two times the number of waffle orders.

_____

LESSON 6-2
One-Step Equations with Rational Coefficients
Practice and Problem Solving: A/B

Solve.

1. $\dfrac{1}{3}n = 4$

    _____

    $n =$ _____

2. $y + 0.4 = 2$

    _____

    $y =$ _____

3. $12 = 0.5a$

    _____

    $a =$ _____

4. $-1 = \dfrac{1}{3}v$

    _____

    $v =$ _____

5. $15.5z = -77.5$

    _____

    $z =$ _____

6. $\dfrac{t}{-11} = 11$

    _____

    $t =$ _____

7. $0.5m = 0.75$

    _____

    $m =$ _____

8. $\dfrac{r}{4} = 250$

    _____

    $r =$ _____

Write each sentence as an equation.

9. Eight less than $\dfrac{1}{3}$ a number n is -13.

    _____

10. A number f multiplied by -12.3 is -73.8.

    _____

Write an equation. Then, solve.

11. During unusually cold weather, the temperature in Miami Beach was 10°C. This was 12 degrees more than in Tallahassee. What is the temperature in Tallahassee?

    _____

12. A swimmer swam 48 kilometers in d days. What is the value of d if the swimmer swam an average of 3.2 kilometers daily?

    _____

13. Fifteen tickets cost $193.75. What is the average cost of each ticket?

    _____

14. A student walks $\dfrac{1}{4}$ mile from her home to the store on her way to a friend's house. If the store is $\dfrac{1}{3}$ of the way to her friend's house, how far is her friend's house from her home?

    _____

Name _____ Date _____ Class_____

One-Step Equations with Rational Coefficients
Reteach

Using Addition to Undo Subtraction

Addition "undoes" subtraction. Adding the same number to both sides of an equation keeps the equation balanced.

$$x - 5 = -6.3$$
$$x - 5 + 5 = -6.3 + 5$$
$$x = -1.3$$

Using Subtraction to Undo Addition

Subtraction "undoes" addition. Subtracting a number from both sides of an equation keeps the equation balanced.

$$n + \frac{3}{4} = -15$$
$$n + \frac{3}{4} - \frac{3}{4} = -15 - \frac{3}{4}$$
$$n = -15\frac{3}{4}$$

Be careful to identify the correct number that is to be added or subtracted from both sides of an equation. The numbers and variables can move around, as the problems show.

Solve using addition or subtraction.

1. $6 = m - \frac{7}{8}$

2. $3.9 + t = 4.5$

3. $10 = -3.1 + j$

_____ _____ _____

Multiplication Undoes Division

To "undo" division, multiply both sides of an equation by the number in the denominator of a problem like this one.

$$\frac{m}{3} = 6$$
$$3 \times \frac{m}{3} = 3 \times 6$$
$$m = 18$$

Division Undoes Multiplication

To "undo" multiplication, divide both sides of an equation by the number that is multiplied by the variable as shown in this problem.

$$4.5p = 18$$
$$\frac{4.5p}{4.5} = \frac{18}{4.5} = 4$$

Notice that decimals and fractions can be handled this way, too.

Solve using division or multiplication.

4. $\frac{y}{2.4} = 5$

5. $0.35w = -7$

6. $-\frac{a}{6} = 1$

_____ _____ _____

LESSON 6-3 Writing Two-Step Equations
Practice and Problem Solving: A/B

Model each two-step operation by drawing algebra tiles.

1. $3m + 5 = 8$

_____

2. $-2x - 3 = 5$.

_____

Write an equation to represent each problem.

3. The sum of fifteen and six times a number t is eighty-one. What is the number?

_____

4. An electrician charges $40 to come to your house. She also charges $55 for each hour that she works. The electrician charges you a total of $190. How many hours does the electrician work at your house? Use h for the number of hours.

_____

5. A taxi charges $1.75 plus a fee of $0.75 for each mile traveled. The total cost of a ride, without a tip, is $4.75. How many miles is the trip? Use m for the number of miles traveled.

_____

Writing Two-Step Equations
Reteach

Many real-world problems look like this:

> **one-time amount** + **number** × **variable** = **total amount**

You can use this pattern to write an equation.

Example:

At the start of a month a customer spends $3 for a reusable coffee cup. She pays $2 each time she has the cup filled with coffee. At the end of the month she has paid $53. How many cups of coffee did she get?

one-time amount:	$3
number × variable:	$2 \times c$ or $2c$, where c is the number of cups of coffee
total amount:	$53

The equation is: $3 + 2c = 53$.

Write an equation to represent each situation.
Each problem can be represented using the form:
> **one-time amount** + **number** × **variable** = **total amount**

1. The sum of twenty-one and five times a number f is 61.

   _____ + _____ = _____

       one-time amount   +   number × variable   =   total amount

2. Seventeen more than seven times a number j is 87.

   _____

3. A customer's total cell phone bill this month is $50.50. The company charges a monthly fee of $18 plus five cents for each call. Use n to represent the number of calls.

   _____

4. A tutor works with a group of students. The tutor charges $40 plus $30 for each student in the group. Today the tutor has s students and charges a total of $220.

   _____

LESSON 6-4

Solving Two-Step Equations
Practice and Problem Solving: A/B

Solve each equation. Cross out each number in the box that matches a solution.

| -18 | -8 | -6 | -4 | -3 | -2 | 2 | 3 | 4 | 6 | 8 | 18 |

1. $5x + 8 = 23$

_____

2. $-2p - 4 = 2$

_____

3. $6a - 11 = 13$

_____

4. $4n + 12 = 4$

_____

5. $9g + 2 = 20$

_____

6. $\frac{k}{6} + 8 = 5$

_____

7. $\frac{s}{3} - 4 = 2$

_____

8. $\frac{c}{2} + 5 = 1$

_____

9. $9 + \frac{a}{6} = 8$

_____

Solve. Check each answer.

10. $3v - 12 = 15$

_____

11. $8 + 5x = -2$

_____

12. $\frac{d}{4} - 9 = -3$

_____

Write an equation to represent the problem. Then solve the equation.

13. Two years of local Internet service costs $685, including the installation fee of $85. What is the monthly fee?

_____

14. The sum of two consecutive numbers is 73. What are the numbers?

_____

LESSON 6-4
Solving Two-Step Equations
Reteach

Here is a key to solving an equation.

Example: Solve $3x - 7 = 8$.

Step 1: • Describe how to form the expression $3x - 7$ from the variable x:
 • Multiply by 3. Then subtract 7.

Step 2: • Write the parts of Step 1 in the reverse order and use inverse operations:
 • Add 7. Then divide by 3.

Step 3: • Apply Step 2 to *both sides* of the original equation.
 • Start with the original equation. $3x - 7 = 8$
 • Add 7 to both sides. $3x = 15$
 • Divide both sides by 3. $x = 5$

Describe the steps to solve each equation. Then solve the equation.

1. $4x + 11 = 19$

_____

2. $-3y + 10 = -14$

_____

3. $\dfrac{r - 11}{3} = -7$

_____

4. $5 - 2p = 11$

_____

5. $\dfrac{2}{3}z + 1 = 13$

_____

6. $\dfrac{w - 17}{9} = 2$

_____

LESSON 7-1

Writing and Solving One-Step Inequalities

Practice and Problem Solving: A/B

Solve each inequality. Graph and check the solution.

1. $\dfrac{e}{2} < 3$ _____

2. $n - 1 > 3$ _____

3. $5 < 3 + w$ _____

4. $8 \le 2m$ _____

5. $r - 4 < 1$ _____

6. $2 \le -1t$ _____

7. $2 \ge s - 2$ _____

8. $2 \ge 5 + p$ _____

Solve each inequality.

9. $\dfrac{1}{5} \le \dfrac{x}{15}$ _____

10. $9 > -r$ _____

11. $-2 + b < 3$ _____

12. $70 - a \ge 25$ _____

Write an inequality for each problem. Then solve.

13. Arthur earned $136 in three weeks. He goes back to school in one more week. He needs at least $189 to buy the new coat that he wants for school. How much must Arthur earn in the next week?

_____

14. Marna is playing a game where you score −5 points each time you guess the correct answer. The goal is to get the lowest score. To win the game, Marna must have a score less than −80 points. How many correct answers does Marna need to win the game?

_____

LESSON
7-1

Writing and Solving One-Step Inequalities
Reteach

When solving an inequality, solve it as if it is an equation. Then decide on the correct inequality sign to put in the answer.

When adding or subtracting a number from each side of an inequality, the sign stays the same. When multiplying or dividing by a positive number, the sign stays the same. When multiplying or dividing by a negative number, the sign changes.

$x + 5 > -5$	$x - 3 \leq 8$	$-2x \geq 8$	Dividing by a negative, so reverse the inequality sign.	$\dfrac{x}{3} < -6$
$x + 5 - 5 > -5 - 5$	$x - 3 + 3 \leq 8 + 3$	$\dfrac{-2x}{-2} \leq \dfrac{8}{-2}$		$\dfrac{x}{(3)}(3) < (-6)(3)$
$x > -10$	$x \leq 11$	$x \leq -4$		$x < -18$

Check:
Think: 0 is a solution because $0 > -10$. Substitute 0 for x to see if your answer checks.

$x + 5 > -5$
$0 + 5 \ ? \ -5$
$5 > -5$ ✓

Check:
Think: 0 is a solution because $0 \leq 11$. Substitute 0 for x to see if your answer checks.

$x - 3 \leq 8$
$0 - 5 \ ? \ 8$
$-5 \leq 8$ ✓

Check:
Think: -6 is a solution because $-6 \leq -4$. Substitute -6 for x to see if your answer checks.

$-2x \geq 8$
$-2 \bullet -6 \ ? \ 8$
$12 \geq 8$ ✓

Check: Think: -21 is a solution because $-21 < -18$. Substitute -21 for x to see if your answer checks.

$\dfrac{x}{3} < -6$
$\dfrac{-21}{3} \ ? \ -6$
$-7 < -6$ ✓

Solve each inequality. Check your work.

1. $n + 6 \geq -3$

_____

2. $-2n < -12$

_____

3. $\dfrac{n}{3} \leq -21$

_____

4. $n - (-3) \geq 7$

_____

5. $-15 + n < -8$

_____

6. $6n > -12$

_____

7. $-6 + n < -9$

_____

8. $\dfrac{n}{-6} > -2$

_____

LESSON 7-2

Writing Two-Step Inequalities
Practice and Problem Solving: A/B

Write an inequality for each description.

1. Ten times a number increased by four is no more than twenty-five.

   _____

2. Thirty subtracted from four times a number is greater than the opposite of ten.

   _____

3. One fourth of the opposite of the difference of five and a number is less than twenty.

   _____

Write a description of each inequality.

4. $-5a + 3 > 1$

   _____

5. $27 - 2b \leq -6$

   _____

6. $\frac{1}{2}(c + 1) \geq 5$

   _____

Use the following situation to complete Exercise 7.

7. The school photography club charges $10 for each photo in its annual pet photo contest. The club wants to save $75 of its earnings for a pizza party. The club members also want to have at least $50 left over after the pizza party to pay for other club expenses. Write an expression for:

   a. how much money the club earns by taking *p* pet photos

      _____

   b. the difference between the amount the club earns and the amount for the pizza party

      _____

   c. Now write a two-step inequality for finding the smallest number of photographs that need to be made to pay for the club's pizza party and have at least $50 left over to pay club expenses.

      _____

LESSON
7-2
Writing Two-Step Inequalities
Reteach

Two-step inequalities involve
- a division or multiplication
- an addition or subtraction.

Step 1
The description indicates whether division or multiplication is involved:

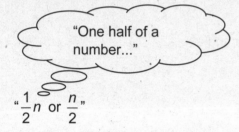

"$\frac{1}{2}n$ or $\frac{n}{2}$"

Step 2
The description indicates whether addition or subtraction is involved:

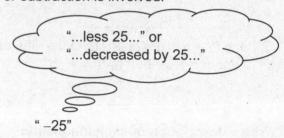

"-25"

Step 3
Combine the two to give two steps:

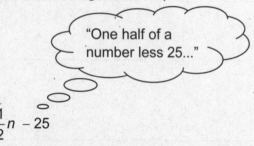

$\frac{1}{2}n - 25$

Step 4
Use an inequality symbol:

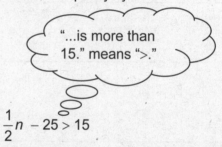

$\frac{1}{2}n - 25 > 15$

Fill in the steps as shown above.

1. Five less than 3 times a number is greater than the opposite of 8.

   Step 1: _____

   Step 2: _____

   Step 3: _____

   Step 4: _____

2. Thirteen plus 5 times a number is no more than 30.

   Step 1: _____

   Step 2: _____

   Step 3: _____

   Step 4: _____

LESSON 7-3

Solving Two-Step Inequalities
Practice and Problem Solving: A/B

Fill in the blanks to show the steps in solving the inequality.

1. $3x - 5 < 19$

$3x - 5 + \underline{} < 19 + \underline{}$

$3x < \underline{}$

$3x \div \underline{} < \underline{} \div \underline{}$

$x < \underline{}$

2. $-2x + 12 < -4$

$-2x + 12 - \underline{} < -4 - \underline{}$

$-2x < \underline{}$

$-2x \div \underline{} > \underline{} \div \underline{}$

$x > \underline{}$

3. Why do the inequality signs stay the same in the last two steps of Exercise 1?

_____

4. Why is the inequality sign reversed in the last two steps of Exercise 2?

_____

Solve the inequalities. Show your work.

5. $-7d + 8 > 29$

6. $12 - 3b < 9$

7. $\dfrac{z}{7} - 6 \geq -5$

_____

_____

_____

_____

_____

_____

8. Fifty students are trying to raise at least $12,500 for a class trip. They have already raised $1,250. How much should each student raise, on average, in order to meet the goal? Write and solve the two-step inequality for this problem.

_____

_____

9. At the end of the day, vegetables at Farm Market sell for $2.00 a pound, and a basket costs $3.50. If Charlene wants to buy a basket and spend no more than $10.00 total, how many pounds of vegetables can she buy? Write and solve the inequality.

_____

_____

Name _____ Date _____ Class_____

LESSON 8-1 Similar Shapes and Scale Drawings
Reteach

The dimensions of a scale model or scale drawing are related to the actual dimensions by a *scale factor*. The **scale factor** is a ratio.

The length of a model car is 9 in. ⟶

The length of the actual car is 162 in. ⟶

$$\frac{9 \text{ in.}}{162 \text{ in.}} = \frac{9 \div 9}{162 \div 9} = \frac{1}{18}$$

$\frac{9}{162}$ can be simplified to $\frac{1}{18}$.

The scale factor is $\frac{1}{18}$.

If you know the scale factor, you can use a proportion to find the dimensions of an actual object or of a scale model or drawing.

- The scale factor of a model train set is $\frac{1}{87}$. A piece of track in the model train set is 8 in. long. What is the actual length of the track?

$$\frac{\text{model length}}{\text{actual length}} = \frac{8}{x} \qquad \frac{8}{x} = \frac{1}{87} \qquad x = 696$$

The actual length of track is 696 inches.

- The distance between 2 cities on a map is 4.5 centimeters. The map scale is 1 cm : 40 mi.

$$\frac{\text{distance on map}}{\text{actual distance}} = \frac{4.5 \text{ cm}}{x \text{ mi}} = \frac{1 \text{ cm}}{40 \text{ mi}} \quad \frac{4.5}{x} = x = 180$$

The actual distance is 180 miles.

Identify the scale factor.

1. Photograph: height 3 in.
   Painting: height 24 in.

   $$\frac{\text{photo height}}{\text{painting height}} = \frac{\text{in.}}{\text{in.}} = \underline{\quad}$$

2. Butterfly: wingspan 20 cm
   Silk butterfly: wingspan 4 cm

   $$\frac{\text{silk butterfly}}{\text{butterfly}} = \frac{\text{cm}}{\text{cm}} = \underline{\quad}$$

Solve.

3. On a scale drawing, the scale factor is $\frac{1}{12}$. A plum tree is 7 inches tall on the scale drawing. What is the actual height of the tree?

   _____

4. On a road map, the distance between 2 cities is 2.5 inches. The map scale is 1 inch:30 miles. What is the actual distance between the cities?

   _____

Original content Copyright © by Houghton Mifflin Harcourt. Additions and changes to the original content are the responsibility of the instructor.

54

LESSON
8-2

Geometric Drawings

Practice and Problem Solving: A/B

Use each set of line segments to sketch a triangle. If a triangle cannot be drawn, explain why.

1.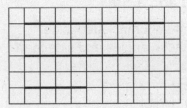

2.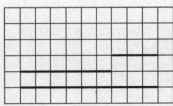

Sketch:

Sketch:

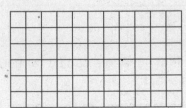

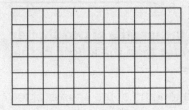

_____

_____

_____

_____

Can each set of line segments form a triangle? Why or why not?

3. $\overline{AB} = \frac{1}{2}$ mile

4. $\overline{DE} = 0.205$ kilometer

$\overline{BC} = \frac{1}{3}$ mile

$\overline{EF} = 0.01$ kilometer

$\overline{AC} = \frac{1}{4}$ mile

$\overline{DF} = 0.02$ kilometer

_____

_____

_____

_____

How many triangles are formed by the angles and sides—unique triangle, more than one triangle, or no triangle?

5.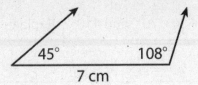

6.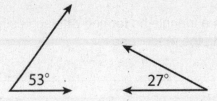

_____

_____

LESSON 8-2 Geometric Drawings
Reteach

In this lesson, you learned two different sets of conditions for drawing a triangle.

Three Sides

Can these three sides form a triangle?

The condition that a triangle can be formed is based on this fact:

The sum of the lengths of two shorter sides is greater than the length of the longest side.

What are the lengths of the shorter sides?

4 and **5** units

What is the length of the longest side?

8 units

Is **4 + 5 > 8**? Yes.

Two Angles and a Side

Why is a common, or included, side needed? Do these angles and side form a triangle?

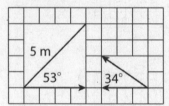

The condition that a triangle can be formed is based on this fact:

The sum of the measures of the angles in a plane triangle is 180 degrees.

What would be the measure of the third angle in a triangle formed from these parts?

$$180° = 53° + 34° + x°$$
$$x° = 180° - 87°$$
$$x = 93°$$

A triangle can be formed, with the angles 53° and 93° having the 5-meter side in common.

Answer the questions about triangle drawings.

1. Can a triangle be formed with three sides of equal length? Explain using the model above.

   _____

   _____

2. Can a triangle be formed with angles having measures of 30°, 70°, and 110°? Explain using the model above.

   _____

   _____

LESSON 8-3

Cross Sections
Practice and Problem Solving: A/B

What is the common set of points for these figures called—an *intersection* or a *cross section*? Place a check mark by the correct name. Describe the geometric figure formed by the common points. Assume that the two figures have more than one point in common.

1. A circle and the lateral surface of a cone.

    Cross section _____   Intersection _____

    Figure formed: _____

2. The edge of a square and the base of a pyramid.

    Cross section _____   Intersection _____

    Figure formed: _____

3. A plane that is perpendicular to the base of a cube and slices through the cube.

    Cross section _____   Intersection _____

    Figure formed: _____

4. A circle with an area bigger than the base of a pyramid and slicing parallel to the base through the pyramid between its apex and its base.

    Cross section _____   Intersection _____

    Figure formed: _____

Name or describe the geometric figure that is shaded. Each shaded region results from a plane passing through the solid.

5.

_____

6.

_____

7.

_____

8.

_____

Name _____ Date _____ Class_____

LESSON 8-3 Cross Sections
Reteach

Cross sections can take a variety of shapes, but they are generally related to the parts of the figures from which they are formed. The angle at which the intersecting plane "cuts" the figure is also a factor in determining the shape of the cross section. However, the cross section is always defined as a plane figure in the situations presented here.

Example 1

When the intersecting plane is *parallel* to the base(s) of the figure, the cross section is often related to the shape of the base. In this cylinder, the cross section is congruent to the bases.

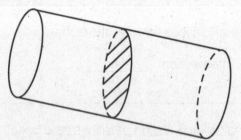

What is the shape of the cross section?
The cross section is a circle that is congruent to each of the bases of the cylinder.

Example 2

When the intersecting plane is *perpendicular* to the base(s) of the figure, the cross section is not always the same shape as the base. In this cylinder, the cross section is a rectangle, not a circle.

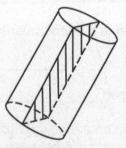

What is the cross section?
A rectangle having a length equal to the height of the cylinder and a width equal to the diameter of the cylinder.

For each solid, draw at least two cross sections with different shapes. Describe the cross sections.

1.

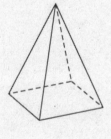

_____

_____

_____

_____

2.

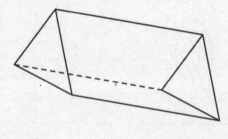

_____

_____

_____

_____

LESSON 8-4

Angle Relationships

Practice and Problem Solving: A/B

For Exercises 1–3, use the figure.

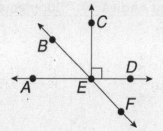

1. Name a pair of vertical angles.

   _____

2. Name a pair of complementary angles.

   _____

3. Name a pair of supplementary angles.

   _____

Use the diagram to find each angle measure.

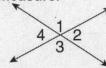

4. If m∠1 = 120°, find m∠3.

   _____

6. If m∠3 = 110°, find m∠2.

   _____

5. If m∠2 = 13°, find m∠4.

   _____

7. If m∠4 = 65°, find m∠1.

   _____

Find the value of *x* in each figure.

8.

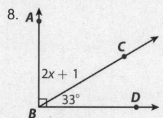

   _____

9.

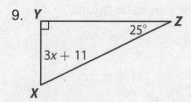

   _____

10.

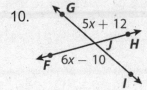

   _____

11.

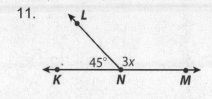

   _____

LESSON 8-4

Angle Relationships

Reteach

Complementary Angles	Supplementary Angles	Vertical Angles
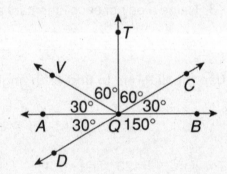	155° 25° C D	a d c b
Two angles whose measures have a sum of 90°.	Two angles whose measures have a sum of 180°.	Intersecting lines form two pairs of vertical angles.

Use the diagram to complete the following.

1. Since ∠AQC and ∠DQB are formed by intersecting lines, $\overrightarrow{AQB}$ and $\overrightarrow{CQD}$, they are:

   _____

2. The sum of the measures of ∠AQV and ∠VQT is: _____
   So, these angles are:

   _____

3. The sum of the measures of ∠AQC and ∠CQB is: _____

   So, these angles are: _____

Find the value of x in each figure.

4.

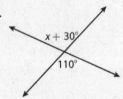

x + 30°

110°

_____

5.

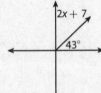

2x + 7

43°

_____

6.

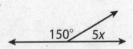

150°   5x

_____

7.

62°

2x + 9

_____

LESSON 9-1

Circumference
Practice and Problem Solving: A/B

Find the circumference of each circle. Use 3.14 or $\frac{22}{7}$ for π. Round to the nearest hundredth, if necessary.

1.
6 in.

_____

2.
9 cm

_____

3.
1.5 ft

_____

4.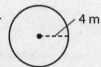
4 m

_____

5.
12 ft

_____

6.
2 yd

_____

7.
7 in.

_____

8.
9 cm

_____

9.
2.5 m

_____

Solve.

10. A circular swimming pool is 21 feet in diameter. What is the circumference of the swimming pool? Use $\frac{22}{7}$ for π.

_____

11. A jar lid has a diameter of 42 millimeters. What is the circumference of the lid? Use $\frac{22}{7}$ for π.

_____

12. A frying pan has a radius of 14 centimeters. What is the circumference of the frying pan? Use $\frac{22}{7}$ for π.

_____

Name _____ Date _____ Class _____

Circumference
Reteach

The distance around a circle is called the **circumference.** To find the circumference of a circle, you need to know the diameter or the radius of the circle.

The ratio of the circumference of any circle to its diameter $\left(\dfrac{C}{d}\right)$

is always the same. This ratio is known as π (pi) and has a value of approximately 3.14.

To find the circumference C of a circle if you know the diameter d, multiply π times the diameter. $C = \pi \bullet d$, or $C \approx 3.14 \bullet d$.

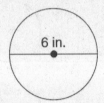
6 in.

$C = \pi \bullet d$
$C \approx 3.14 \bullet d$
$C \approx 3.14 \bullet 6$
$C \approx 18.84$
The circumference is about 18.8 in. to the nearest tenth.

The diameter of a circle is twice as long as the radius r, or $d = 2r$.
To find the circumference if you know the radius, replace d with $2r$ in the formula. $C = \pi \bullet d = \pi \bullet 2r$

Find the circumference given the diameter.

1. $d = 9$ cm
   $C = \pi \bullet d$
   $C \approx 3.14 \bullet$ _____

   $C \approx$ _____
   The circumference is _____ cm to the nearest tenth of a centimeter.

Find the circumference given the radius.

2. $r = 13$ in.
   $C = \pi \bullet 2r$
   $C \approx 3.14 \bullet (2 \bullet$ _____ $)$

   $C \approx 3.14 \bullet$ _____

   $C \approx$ _____
   The circumference is _____ in. to the nearest tenth of an inch.

Find the circumference of each circle to the nearest tenth. Use 3.14 for π.

3.
13 cm

_____

4.
5 ft

_____

5.
1.5 in.

_____

Name _____ Date _____ Class_____

 LESSON 9-2

Area of Circles

Practice and Problem Solving: A/B

Find the area of each circle to the nearest tenth. Use 3.14 for π.

1.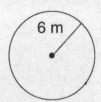

6 m

A   113 m^2 C   354.9 m^2
B   37.7 m^2 D   452.16 m^2

2.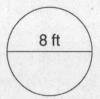

8 ft

A   201 ft^2 C   25.1 ft^2
B   50.2 ft^2 D   157.8 ft^2

3.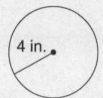

4 in.

_____

4.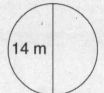

14 m

_____

5.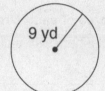

9 yd

_____

Find the area of each circle in terms of π.

6.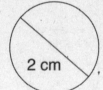

2 cm

_____

7.

7.4 cm

_____

8.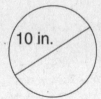

10 in.

_____

9.

22 mm

_____

10.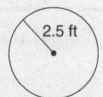

2.5 ft

_____

11.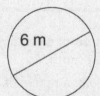

6 m

_____

LESSON 9-2

Area of Circles

Reteach

The area of a circle is found by using the formula $A = \pi r^2$. To find the area, first determine the radius. Square the radius and multiply the result by π. This gives you the exact area of the circle.

Example:

Find the area of the circle in terms of π.

10 cm

The diameter is 10 cm. The radius is half the diameter, or 5 cm.
Area is always given in square units.

$$5^2 = 25$$
$$A = 25\pi \text{ cm}^2$$

Find the area of each circle in terms of π.

1. A vinyl album with a diameter of 16 inches.

2. A compact disc with a diameter of 120 mm.

_____

_____

Sometimes it is more useful to use an estimate of π to find your answer.
Use 3.14 as an estimate for π.

Example:

Find the area of the circle. Use 3.14 for π and round your answer to the nearest tenth.

The radius is 2.8 cm.
Area is always given in square units.

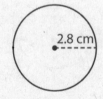

2.8 cm

$$2.8^2 = 7.84$$
$$A = 7.84\pi \text{ cm}^2$$
$$A = 7.84 \times 3.14 \text{ cm}^2$$
$$A = 24.6176 \text{ cm}^2$$

Rounded to the nearest tenth, the area is 24.6 cm².

Find the area of each circle. Use 3.14 for π and round your answer to the nearest tenth.

3. A pie with a radius of 4.25 inches.

4. A horse ring with a radius of 10 yards.

_____

_____

5. A round pond with a diameter of 24 m.

6. A biscuit with a diameter of 9.2 cm.

_____

_____

LESSON 9-3

Area of Composite Figures
Practice and Problem Solving: A/B

Estimate the area of each figure. Each square represents 1 square foot.

1.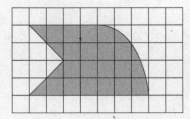

2.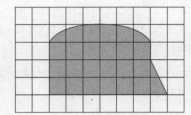

_____   _____

Find the area of each figure. Use 3.14 for π.

3.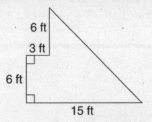

4.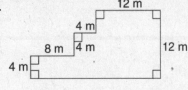

5.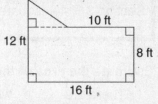

_____   _____   _____

6.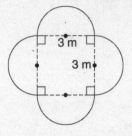

7.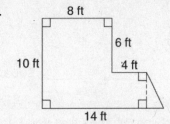

8.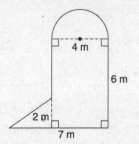

_____   _____   _____

9. Marci is going to use tile to cover her terrace. How much tile does she need?

_____

LESSON
9-3
Area of Composite Figures
Reteach

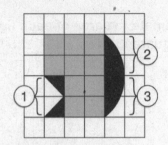

When an irregular figure is on graph paper, you can estimate its area by counting whole squares and parts of squares. Follow these steps.

- Count the number of whole squares. There are 10 whole squares.

- Combine parts of squares to make whole squares or half-squares.

Section 1 = 1 square

Section 2 $\approx 1\frac{1}{2}$ squares

Section 3 $\approx 1\frac{1}{2}$ squares

- Add the whole and partial squares

$$10 + 1 + 1\frac{1}{2} + 1\frac{1}{2} = 14$$

The area is about 14 square units.

Estimate the area of the figure.

1. There are _____ whole squares in the figure.

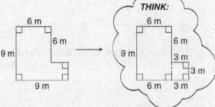

Section 1 $\approx$ _____ square(s)

Section 2 = _____ square(s)

Section 3 = _____ square(s)

$A =$ _____ + _____ + _____ + _____ = _____ square units

You can break a composite figure into shapes that you know. Then use those shapes to find the area.

A (rectangle) $= 9 \times 6 = 54$ m^2

A (square) $= 3 \bullet 3 = 9$ m^2

A (composite figure) $= 54 + 9 = 63$ m^2

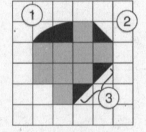

Find the area of the figure.

2. A (rectangle) = _____ ft^2

A (triangle) = _____ ft^2

A (composite figure) = _____ + _____ = _____ ft^2

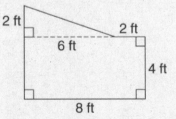

LESSON 9-4

Solving Surface Area Problems
Practice and Problem Solving: A/B

Find the surface area of each solid figure.

1.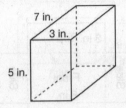
7 in.
3 in.
5 in.

_____

2.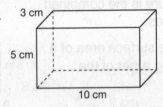
3 cm
5 cm
10 cm

_____

3.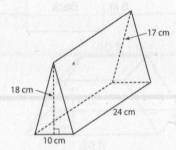
17 cm
18 cm
24 cm
10 cm

_____

4.
10 ft
20 ft
30 ft
10 ft
36 ft
24 ft

_____

Use the situation below to complete Exercises 5–6.

Cydney built a display stand out of two cubes. The larger cube is 8 inches on each side. The smaller cube is 4 inches on each side. She painted the display stand <u>after</u> she put the two cubes together. She did NOT paint the bottom of the display stand. What was the total area she painted?

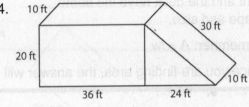
4 in.
8 in.

5. Explain your plan for solving the problem.

_____

_____

6. Solve the problem.

_____

_____

LESSON 9-5

Solving Volume Problems
Reteach

The **volume** of a solid figure is the number of cubic units inside the figure.

A prism is a solid figure that has length, width, and height.

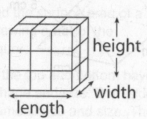

height

width

length

Each small cube represents one cubic unit.

one cubic unit

Volume is measured in cubic units, such as in^3, cm^3, ft^3, and m^3.

The volume of a solid figure is the product of the area of the base (B) and the height (h).

$$V = Bh$$

Rectangular Prism	Triangular Prism	Trapezoidal Prism
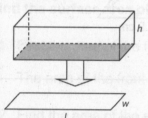	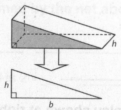	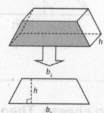
The base is a rectangle. To find the area of the base, use $B = lw$.	The base is a triangle. To find the area of the base, use $B = \frac{1}{2}bh$.	The base is a trapezoid. To find the area of the base, use $B = \frac{1}{2}(b_1 + b_2)h$.

Find the volume of each figure.

1.

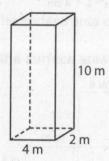

10 m

2 m

4 m

_____

2.

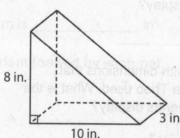

8 in.

10 in.

3 in.

_____

3.

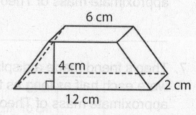

6 cm

4 cm

12 cm

2 cm

_____

Name _____ Date _____ Class_____

LESSON 10-1

Comparing Data Displayed in Dot Plots
Practice and Problem Solving: A/B

Find the values for each dot plot.

1.

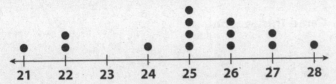

Range: _____ Median: _____ Mode: _____

_____ _____ _____

2.

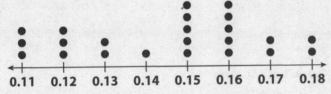

Range: _____ Median: _____ Mode: _____

_____ _____ _____

Compare the dot plots by answering the questions.

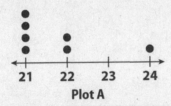

Plot A   **Plot B**

3. How do the ranges compare?   4. Compare the number of elements.

_____   _____

5. How do the modes compare?   6. How do the medians compare?

_____   _____

7. Describe the distribution of the dots in each plot.

_____

LESSON 10-1

Comparing Data Displayed in Dot Plots
Reteach

A **dot plot** is a visual way to show the spread of data. A number line is used to show every data point in a set.

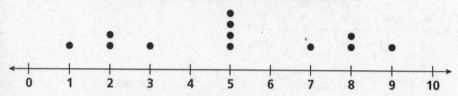

Paula: Goals Scored Per Game This Season

You can describe the shape of the data plot.

- The center, with an equal number of dots on each side, is at 5.
- The data values start at 1 and end at 9.
- Most of the dots occur at 5.
- The mean, median, and mode are all 5.

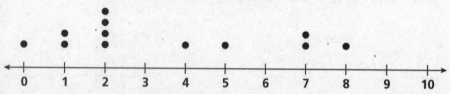

Paula: Goals Scored Per Game Last Season

Data sets are not always evenly spread with most in the middle. The data may cluster more to the left or right of center.

- This dot plot shows that most of the data are left of center.
- The data values start at 0 and end at 8.
- Most of the dots occur at 2.
- The mean, median, and mode vary.

Describe the shape of the data distribution for the dot plot.

1.

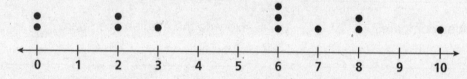

Jaime: Goals Scored Per Game This Season

_____

_____

_____

LESSON 10-2 # Comparing Data Displayed in Box Plots

Practice and Problem Solving: A/B

1. Use the data to make a box-and-whisker plot. 24, 32, 35, 18, 20, 36, 12

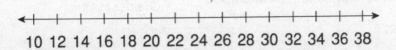

10 12 14 16 18 20 22 24 26 28 30 32 34 36 38

The box-and-whisker plot shows the test scores of two students. Use the box-and-whisker plot for Exercises 2–5.

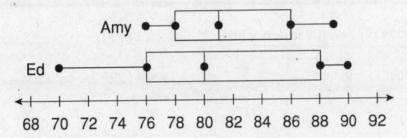

Amy

Ed

68 70 72 74 76 78 80 82 84 86 88 90 92

2. Which student has the greater median test score? _____

3. Which student has the greater interquartile range of test scores? _____

4. Which student has the greater range of test scores? _____

5. Which student appears to have more predictable test scores? Explain your answer.

_____

_____

The box-and-whisker plot shows prices of hotel rooms in two beach towns. Use the box-and-whisker plot for Exercises 6–8.

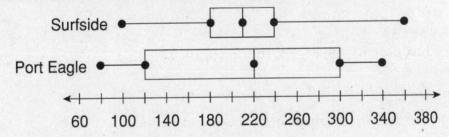

Surfside

Port Eagle

60   100   140   180   220   260   300   340   380

6. Which town has the greater median room price? _____

7. Which town has the greater interquartile range of room prices? _____

8. Which town appears to have more predictable room prices? Explain your answer.

_____

_____

Comparing Data Displayed in Box Plots

LESSON 10-2

Reteach

A **box plot** separates a set of data into four equal parts.

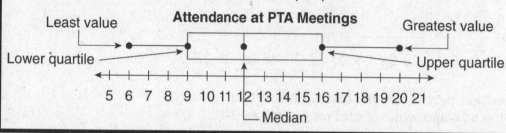

Attendance at PTA Meetings

Least value

Lower quartile

Greatest value

Upper quartile

Median

Use the data to create a box plot on the number line: 35, 24, 25, 38, 31, 20, 27

1. Order the data from least to greatest.

    _____

2. Find the least value, the greatest value, and the median.

    _____

3. The **lower quartile** is the median of the lower half of the data.
   The **upper quartile** is the median of the upper half of the data.
   Find the lower and upper quartiles.

   Lower quartile: _____   Upper quartile: _____

4. Above the number line, plot points for the numbers you found in
   Exercises 2 and 3. Draw a box around the quartiles and the median.
   Draw a line from the least value to the lower quartile. Draw a line from
   the upper quartile to the greatest value.

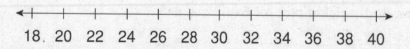

    18   20   22   24   26   28   30   32   34   36   38   40

Use the data to create a box plot: 63, 69, 61, 74, 78, 72, 68, 70, 65

5. Order the data. _____

6. Find the least and greatest values, the median, the lower and
   upper quartiles.

   _____

7. Draw the box plot above the number line.

    60   62   64   66   68   70   72   74   76   78   80

Using Statistical Measures to Compare Populations

Practice and Problem Solving: A/B

The table shows the ages of random samples of 10 students at two different secondary schools.

Mountain View	Ocean View
11, 14, 13, 13, 19, 18, 15, 16, 16, 14	13, 14, 15, 14, 18, 17, 12, 18, 11, 14

1. What is the mean and the mean absolute deviation of the ages of the sample of students at Mountain View?

   Mean: _____ MAD: _____

2. What is the mean and the mean absolute deviation of the ages of the sample of students at Ocean View?

   Mean: _____ MAD: _____

3. What is the difference of the means?

   _____

4. What is the difference of the means as a multiple of the mean absolute deviations?

   _____

The box plots show the distributions of mean incomes of 10 samples of 10 adults from each of two cities, A and B.

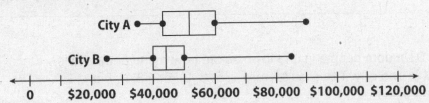

5. What can you say about any comparison of the incomes of the two populations? Explain.

   _____

   _____

   _____

   _____

   _____

LESSON
10-3
Using Statistical Measures to Compare Populations
Reteach

The Thompson family of 5 has a mean weight of 150 pounds. The
Wilson family of 5 has a mean weight of 154 pounds. Based on that
information, you might think that the Thompson family members
and the Wilson family members were about the same weight.
The actual values are shown in the tables below.

Thompson Family
55, 95, 154, 196, 250

Wilson Family
132, 153, 155, 161, 169

By comparing the means to a measure of variability we can get a better
sense of how the two families differ.

The Thompson family's mean absolute deviation is 60. The Wilson
family's mean absolute deviation is 9.2.

The difference of the two means is 4. This is 0.07 times the mean
absolute deviation for the Thompson family, but 0.4 times the mean
absolute deviation for the Wilson family.

**The tables show the number of pets owned by 10 students in a rural
town and 10 students in a city.**

Rural Town
3, 16, 3, 6, 4, 5, 0, 2, 12, 8

City
2, 0, 1, 2, 4, 0, 1, 0, 0, 1

1. What is the difference of the means as a multiple of each range?

_____

A survey of 10 random people in one town asked how many phone calls
they received in one day. The results were 1, 5, 3, 2, 4, 0, 3, 6, 8 and 2.
The mean was 3.4.

Taking 3 more surveys of 10 random people added more data. The means
of the new surveys were 1.2, 2.8, and 2.2. Based on the new data, Ann's
assumption that 3.4 calls was average seems to be incorrect.

2. Raul surveyed 4 groups of 10 random people in a second town to ask
how many phone calls they receive. The means of the 4 groups were
3.2, 1.4, 1.2, and 2.1. What can you say about the number of phone
calls received in the towns surveyed by Ann and Raul?

_____

_____

**LESSON
11-1**

Populations and Samples

Practice and Problem Solving: A/B

Name the *population* and the *sample* in each exercise. Explain your answer.

1. The number of roadrunners born within a 50-mile radius of Lubbock.

2. The cars traveling at 75 kilometers per hour between Beaumont and Lufkin.

_____   _____

Name the sampling method that will best represent the whole population in each situation. Explain your answer.

3. Student satisfaction with the middle school cafeteria.

   Method A: Survey 40 students in two seventh-grade math classes. 72 percent are satisfied with the food in the cafeteria.

   Method B: Survey 65 students from a list of all students in the school. 85 percent are satisfied with the food in the cafeteria.

   Method _____ best represents the whole population of the school.

_____

4. Predicted winner in an election for town mayor.

   Method C: Telephone 100 randomly-chosen voters who live in the town. 54 percent plan to vote for the incumbent mayor.

   Method D: Telephone 70 people who have lived in the town for more than 25 years. 45 percent plan to vote for the incumbent mayor.

   Method _____ best represents the whole population of the town's voters.

_____

Which of these may be biased samples? Explain your answer.

5. A town official surveys 50 people in a library to decide if town residents want the library services and facilities expanded.

_____

6. A cable television company randomly calls 200 customers and asks them if they are satisfied with their service.

_____

Name _____ Date _____ Class _____

Populations and Samples
Reteach

Survey topic: number of books read by seventh-graders
in Richmond

A **population** is the whole group that is being studied.	*Population*: all seventh-graders in Richmond
A **sample** is a part of the population.	*Sample*: all seventh graders at Jefferson Middle School
A **random sample** is a sample in which each member of the population has a random chance of being chosen. A random sample is a better representation of a population than a non-random sample.	*Random sample*: Have a computer select every tenth name from an alphabetical list of each seventh-grader in Richmond.
A **biased sample** is a sample that does not truly represent a population.	*Biased sample*: all of the seventh-graders in Richmond who are enrolled in honors English classes.

Tell if each sample is biased. Explain your answer.

1. An airline surveys passengers from a flight that is on time to determine if passengers on all flights are satisfied.

   _____

2. A newspaper randomly chooses 100 names from its subscriber database and then surveys those subscribers to find if they read the restaurant reviews.

   _____

3. The manager of a bookstore sends a survey to 150 customers who were randomly selected from a customer list.

   _____

4. A team of researchers surveys 200 people at a multiplex movie theater to find out how much money state residents spend on entertainment.

   _____

LESSON 11-2

Making Inferences from a Random Sample
Practice and Problem Solving: A/B

What can you infer about the population from each data set represented below?

1.

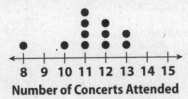

Number of Concerts Attended

2.

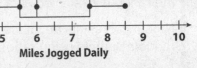

Miles Jogged Daily

_____   _____

The box plots show the distribution of grade-level test scores of 20 students in School A and 20 students in School B. Use the box plots to do Exercises 3–5. Answer True or False for each statement.

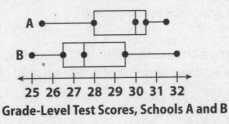

Grade-Level Test Scores, Schools A and B

3. The median score at School A is higher than School B.

4. The range of scores at School B is less than the range of scores at School A.

_____   _____

5. 25% of the students at School A got a score greater than 25 but less than or equal to 28.

_____

Solve.

6. A seventh-grade student chooses a random sample of 50 out of 400 students. He finds that 7 students have traveled outside the United States. The student claims that over 50 of the 400 students have likely traveled outside the United States. Is the student correct? Explain.

_____

7. A metal-fabricating company produces 150,000 souvenir tokens each year. In a random sample of 400 tokens, 3 have stamping errors. Predict the total number of coins that will have stamping errors in a year.

_____

LESSON 11-2
Making Inferences from a Random Sample
Reteach

Once a **random sample** of a **population** has been selected, it can be used to make inferences about the population as a whole. **Dot plots** of the randomly selected data are useful in visualizing trends in a population.

Numerical results about the population can often be obtained from the random sample using **ratios** or **proportions** as these examples show.

Making inferences from a dot plot
The dot plot shows a random sample of 20 shipments of light bulbs. What will be the median number of defective light bulbs in a population of 400 shipments?

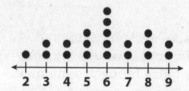

Defective Light Bulbs per Shipment

Solution In this dot plot, the median number of defective light bulbs is 6. Set up a proportion to find the median number of defective light bulbs predicted for 400 shipments:

$$\frac{\text{sample}}{\text{population}} = \frac{20}{400}$$

$$\frac{20}{400} = \frac{6}{x}$$

$$\frac{1}{20} = \frac{6}{x}$$

$$x = 120$$

So, 120 defective light bulbs is the median number of defective light bulbs predicted for the population.

1. In a random sample, 3 of 400 computer chips are defective. Based on the sample, how many chips out of 100,000 would you expect to be defective?

_____

2. In a sample 5 of 800 T-shirts were defective. Based on this sample, in a production run of 250,000 T-shirts, how many would you expect to be defective?

_____

Generating Random Samples

Practice and Problem Solving: A/B

Use the description below to complete Exercises 1–3.

In a set of 1,000 integers from 1 to 1,000, an integer chosen at random on a single trial should be an integer from 1 to 25 about 25 out of every 1,000 trials, or one out of every 40 integers selected.

1. A sample of 5 integers selected is shown. Does this sample represent the general rule for picking an integer from 1 to 25 in the population of integers from 1 to 1,000? Explain.

Trial 1	406
Trial 2	734
Trial 3	44
Trial 4	340
Trial 5	996

_____

2. How many integers between 1 and 25 would you expect to appear in a sample of 80 trials? Explain.

_____

3. The following integers from 1 to 25 appeared when a sample of 50 integers was taken from the list of the integers from 1 to 1,000.

   12, 21, and 16

   Is this sample of 50 trials more or less than what was expected for the population as a whole? Explain.

_____

Use the description below to complete Exercises 4–5.

A manufacturer of flea collars for animals that weigh less than 5 kilograms injects the collars with 15 milligrams of a biocide that only acts on fleas. The manufacturer will release a collar that has no less than 14 milligrams and no more than 16 milligrams of insecticide. The following list shows the result of sampling 36 collars from an actual production run of 720 collars.

   17, 14, 14, 16, 14, 15, 15, 15, 16, 14, 16, 14, 15, 15, 15, 16, 13, 13,

   13, 13, 13, 14, 14, 13, 17, 14, 15, 13, 14, 15, 16, 17, 14, 17, 14, 15

4. How many flea collars out of a production run of 720 collars would be acceptable to ship according to this sample? Explain your reasoning.

_____

5. How many flea collars out of a production run of 720 flea collars would have too much biocide and could not be shipped? Explain your reasoning.

_____

LESSON 11-3
Generating Random Samples
Reteach

A *random sample* of equally-likely *events* can be generated with random-number programs on computers or by reading random numbers from random-number tables in mathematics textbooks that are used in the study of statistics and probability.

In your math class, random samples can be modeled using coins or number cubes. For example, consider the random sample that consists of the sum of the numbers on two number cubes.

Example 1 ———→

Generate 10 random samples of the sum of the numbers on the faces of two number cubes.

Solution

Rolling the number cubes gives these random samples:
2, 6, 6, 4, 3, 11, 11, 8, 7, and 10

Example 2 ———→

What are the different *possible* outcomes from rolling the two number cubes in Example 1? Write the outcomes as sums.

Solution

List the outcomes as ordered pairs:
(1, 1), (1, 2), (1, 3), (1, 4), (1, 5), (1, 6),
(2, 1), (2, 2), (2, 3), (2, 4), (2, 5), (2, 6),
(3, 1), (3, 2), (3, 3), (3, 4), (3, 5), (3, 6),
(4, 1), (4, 2), (4, 3), (4, 4), (4, 5), (4, 6),
(5, 1), (5, 2), (5, 3), (5, 4), (5, 5), (5, 6),
(6, 1), (6, 2), (6, 3), (6, 4), (6, 5), (6, 6)

Then, write the sums of the ordered pairs:
2, 3, 4, 5, 6, 7, 3, 4, 5, 6, 7, 8, 4, 5, 6, 7, 8,
9, 5, 6, 7, 8, 9, 10, 6, 7, 8, 9, 10, 11, 7, 8, 9,
10, 11, and 12

Example 3 ———→

How do the frequency of the outcomes of the 10 random samples in Example 1 compare with the frequency of their sums in Example 2?

Solution

In Example 1, there is one each of 2, 3, 4, 7, 8, and 10, two 6's, and two 11's. In Example 3, there is one 2, two 3's, three 4's, four 5's, five 6's, six 7's, five 8's, four 9's, three 10's, two 11's, and one 12.

Answer the questions about the examples.

1. How do the random samples compare with the predicted number of outcomes?

2. How do you think the outcomes in 100 random samples would compare with the expected results?

LESSON 12-1

Probability

Practice and Problem Solving: A/B

Determine the probability of each event. Write *impossible, unlikely, as likely as not, likely,* **or** *certain.* **Then, tell whether the probability is 0, close to 0, $\frac{1}{2}$, close to 1, or 1.**

1. randomly picking a blue card from a bag containing all blue cards

   _____

2. rolling an odd number on a number cube containing numbers 1 through 6

   _____

3. picking a red marble from 4 white marbles and 7 green marbles

   _____

Find each probability. Write your answer in simplest form.

4. A bag holds 6 tiles: 2 lettered and 4 numbered. Without looking, you choose a tile. What is the probability of drawing a number? _____

5. The names Phil, Angelica, Yolanda, Mimi, and Ed are on slips of paper in a hat. A name is drawn without looking. What is the probability of **not** drawing Ed? _____

6. A standard deck of cards contains 13 of each suit: red hearts, red diamonds, black clubs, and black spades. What is the probability of drawing a red card without looking? _____

A board game includes the 9 cards below.

Move back 2.   Move up 1.   Move up 4.   Move back 3.   Move up 3.   Move up 6.   Move back 2.   Move up 5.   Move up 2.

7. Mia says the probability of moving back is the same as the probability of moving up. Is she correct? What is the probability of moving back? Explain.

   _____

8. Gavin needs to move up more than 4 spaces to win the game. Is he likely to win on his next turn? What is the probability that he will **not** win on his next turn? Explain.

   _____

LESSON
12-2

Experimental Probability of Simple Events
Reteach

Experimental probability is an estimate of the probability that a particular event will happen.

It is called *experimental* because it is based on data collected from experiments or observations.

$$\text{Experimental probability} \approx \frac{\text{number of times a particular event happens}}{\text{total number of trials}}$$

JT is practicing his batting. The pitcher makes 12 pitches. JT hits 8 of the pitches. What is the experimental probability that JT will hit the next pitch?

- A favorable outcome is hitting the pitch.

- The number of favorable outcomes is the number JT hit: 8.

- The number of trials is the total number of pitches: 12.

- The experimental probability that JT will hit the next pitch is $\frac{8}{12} = \frac{2}{3}$.

1. Ramon plays outfield. In the last game, 15 balls were hit in his direction. He caught 12 of them. What is the experimental probability that he will catch the next ball hit in his direction?

   a. What is the number of favorable events? _____

   b. What is the total number of trials? _____

   c. What is the experimental probability that Ramon will catch the next ball hit in his direction?

   _____

2. In one inning Tori pitched 9 strikes and 5 balls. What is the experimental probability that the next pitch she throws will be a strike?

   a. What is the number of favorable events? _____

   b. What is the total number of trials? _____

   c. What is the experimental probability that the next pitch Tori throws will be a strike?

   _____

3. Tori threw 5 pitches for one batter. Kevin, the catcher, caught 4 of those pitches. What is the experimental probability that Kevin will **not** catch the next pitch? Show your work.

   _____

   _____

Name _____ Date _____ Class_____

Experimental Probability of Compound Events
Practice and Problem Solving: A/B

Solve.

1. A coin was tossed and a spinner with three equal sections numbered
   1 to 3 was spun. The results are shown in the table.

	Heads	Tails
1	53	65
2	49	71
3	54	62

   What is the experimental probability that the next toss and spin will
   result in 3 and Tails?

   _____

2. A receptionist recorded the number of people who took an elevator up
   from his floor and the number who took an elevator down. He also
   noted the number of men and women. The table shows the results.

	Elevator Up	Elevator Down
Men	36	43
Women	39	42

   What is the experimental probability that the next person will be a
   woman taking the elevator up?

   _____

3. Sandwich shop customers can choose the bread and meat they want.
   The table shows the sandwiches that were sold on a given day.

	White Bread	Wheat Bread
Ham	22	24
Turkey	21	22
Tuna	25	23

   What is the experimental probability that the next sandwich sold will be
   tuna on wheat bread?

   _____

4. A store sells a coat in three sizes: small, medium, and large. The coat
   comes in red, navy, and tan. Sales numbers are shown in the table.

	Small	Medium	Large
Red	18	21	19
Navy	24	22	20
Tan	19	25	22

   What is the experimental probability that the next coat sold is **not** a
   large navy?

   _____

LESSON 12-3

Experimental Probability of Compound Events
Reteach

A **compound event** includes two or more simple events.

The possible outcomes of flipping a coin are heads and tails.

A spinner is divided into 4 equal sections, each one a different color. The possible outcomes of spinning are red, yellow, blue, and green.

If you toss the coin and spin the spinner, there are 8 possible outcomes.

2 possible **coin outcomes**

4 possible **spinner outcomes**

	Red	Yellow	Blue	Green
Heads	9	11	11	14
Tails	10	12	7	6

8 possible **compound outcomes**

To find the experimental probability that the next trial will have an outcome of Tails and Blue:

a. Find the number of times Tails and Blue was the outcome: 7.

b. Find the total number of trials: $9 + 11 + 11 + 14 + 10 + 12 + 7 + 6 = 80$.

c. Write a ratio of the number of tails and blue outcomes to the number of trials: $\frac{7}{80}$.

A store hands out yogurt samples: peach, vanilla, and strawberry. Each flavor comes in regular or low-fat. By 2 P.M. the store has given out these samples:

	Peach	Vanilla	Strawberry
Regular	16	19	30
Low-fat	48	32	55

Use the table to answer the questions.

1. What is the total number of samples given out? _____

2. What is the experimental probability that the next sample will be regular vanilla?

   _____

3. What is the experimental probability that the next sample will be strawberry?

   _____

4. What is the experimental probability that the next sample will **not** be peach?

   _____

Name _____ Date _____ Class_____

Making Predictions with Experimental Probability

Practice and Problem Solving: A/B

Make a prediction based on experimental probability.

1. A bowler knocks down at least 6 pins 70 percent of the time. Out of 200 rolls, how many times can you predict the bowler will knock down at least 6 pins?

_____

2. A tennis player hits a serve that cannot be returned 45 percent of the time. Out of 300 serves, how many can you predict will not be returned?

_____

3. West Palm Beach, Florida, gets rain about 16 percent of the time. On how many days out of 400 can residents of West Palm Beach predict they will get rain?

_____

4. Rob notices that 55 percent of the people leaving the supermarket choose plastic bags instead of paper bags. Out of 600 people, how many can Rob predict will carry plastic bags?

_____

5. A baseball player reaches base 35 percent of the time. How many times can he expect to reach base in 850 at-bats?

_____

6. Fredericka can make 65 percent of her shots from the free-throw line. If she shoots 75 times, how many shots can she expect to make?

_____

7. In a current-events class, a professor predicted that at least 78 percent of students prefer getting their news from a digital source rather than from a print source. He polled 3 classes. The results are shown in the table below.

	Class 1	Class 2	Class 3
Digital	20	14	30
Print	5	10	7

In which class(es) did his prediction hold true? Explain.

_____

Making Predictions with Experimental Probability

LESSON 12-4

Reteach

When you have information about previous events, you can use that information to predict what will happen in the future.

If you can throw a basketball into the basket 3 out of 5 times, you can predict you will make 6 baskets in 10 tries. If you try 15 times, you will make 9 baskets. You can use a proportion or multiply to make predictions.

A. Use a proportion.

A survey found that 8 of 10 people chose apples as their favorite fruit. If you ask 100 people, how many can you predict will choose apples as their favorite fruit?

$$\frac{8}{10} = \frac{x}{100}$$

Write a proportion. *8 out of 10 is how many out of 100?*

$$\frac{8}{10} = \frac{x}{100}$$
$$\underbrace{}_{\times 10}$$
$$x = 80$$

Since 10 times 10 is 100, multiply 8 times 10 to find the value of *x*.

You can predict that 80 of the people will choose apples as their favorite fruit.

B. Multiply.

Eric's baseball coach calculated that Eric hits the ball 49 percent of the time. If Eric receives 300 pitches this season, how many times can Eric predict that he will hit the ball?

$$0.49 \times 300 = x$$
$$147 = x$$

Eric can predict that he will hit the ball 147 times.

Solve.

1. On average, 25 percent of the dogs who go to ABC Veterinarian need a rabies booster. If 120 dogs visit ABC Veterinarian, how many of them will likely need a rabies booster?

   Set up a proportion: $\dfrac{\rule{1cm}{0.4pt}}{100} = \dfrac{x}{\rule{1cm}{0.4pt}}$

   Solve for *x*: $x = $ _____

   _____ dogs will likely need a rabies booster.

2. About 90 percent of seventh graders prefer texting to emailing. In a sample of 550 seventh graders, how many do you predict will prefer texting?

   $0.9 \times 550 = $ _____

   _____ seventh graders will likely prefer texting.

LESSON 13-1

Theoretical Probability of Simple Events
Practice and Problem Solving: A/B

Find the probability for each event.

1. tossing a number cube numbered from 1 to 6 and getting an even number that is greater than or equal to 2

   _____

2. tossing a number cube numbered from 1 to 6 and getting an odd number that is less than or equal to 3

   _____

3. randomly selecting a seventh grader from a school that has 250 sixth graders, 225 seventh graders, and 275 eighth graders

   _____

4. without looking, **not** picking a red hat from a box that holds 20 red hats, 30 blue hats, 15 green hats, and 25 white hats

   _____

Match each event to its likelihood.

5. rolling a number greater than 6 on a number cube labeled 1 through 6   _____   A. likely

6. flipping a coin and getting heads   _____   B. unlikely

7. drawing a red or blue marble from a bag of red marbles and blue marbles   _____   C. as likely as not

8. spinning a number less than 3 on a spinner with 8 equal sections labeled 1 through 8   _____   D. impossible

9. rolling a number less than 6 on a number cube labeled 1 through 6   _____   E. certain

Use the information to find probabilities in 10–13.

At a school health fair, individual pieces of fruit are placed in paper bags and distributed to students randomly. There are 20 apples, 15 apricots, 25 bananas, 25 pears, and 30 peaches.

10. the probability of getting an apple _____

11. the probability of **not** getting a pear _____

12. the probability of **not** getting an apple _____

13. the probability of getting an orange _____

LESSON 13-1 Theoretical Probability of Simple Events
Reteach

The probability, P, of an event is a ratio.
It can be written as a fraction, decimal, or percent.

$$P(\text{probability of an event}) = \frac{\text{the number of outcomes of an event}}{\text{the total number of all events}}$$

Example 1

There are 20 red and green apples in a bag. The probability of randomly picking a red apple is 0.4. How many red apples are in the bag? How many green apples?

Total number of events ———► 2

Probability, P: $0.4 = \dfrac{\text{number of red apples}}{20}$

So:

number of red apples $= 0.4 \times 20 = 8$

number of green apples $= 20 - 8 = 12$

There are 8 red apples and 12 green apples.

Example 2

A bag contains 1 red marble, 2 blue marbles, and 3 green marbles.

The probability of picking a red marble is $\dfrac{1}{6}$.

To find the probability of **not** picking a red marble, subtract the probability of picking a red marble from 1.

$$P = 1 - \frac{1}{6} = \frac{5}{6}$$

The probability of not picking a red marble from the bag is $\dfrac{5}{6}$.

Solve.

1. A model builder has 30 pieces of balsa wood in a box. Four pieces are 15 inches long, 10 pieces are 12 inches long, and the rest are 8 inches long. What is the probability the builder will pull an 8-inch piece from the box without looking?

   _____

2. There are 30 bottles of fruit juice in a cooler. Some are orange juice, others are cranberry juice, and the rest are other juices. The probability of randomly grabbing one of the other juices is 0.6. How many bottles of orange juice and cranberry juice are in the cooler?

   _____

3. There are 13 dimes and 7 pennies in a cup.

   a. What is the probability of drawing a penny out without looking?
   _____

   b. What is the probability of **not** drawing a penny? _____

4. If $P(\text{event } A) = 0.25$, what is $P(\textbf{not} \text{ event } A)$? _____

5. If $P(\textbf{not} \text{ event } B) = 0.95$, what is $P(\text{event } B)$? _____

LESSON 13-2

Theoretical Probability of Compound Events
Practice and Problem Solving: A/B

Use the table of probabilities to answer questions 1–3.

	Burrito	Taco	Wrap
Cheese	$P = \dfrac{1}{9}$	$P = \dfrac{1}{9}$	$P = \dfrac{1}{9}$
Salsa	$P = \dfrac{1}{9}$	$P = \dfrac{1}{9}$	$P = \dfrac{1}{9}$
Veggie	$P = \dfrac{1}{9}$	$P = \dfrac{1}{9}$	$P = \dfrac{1}{9}$

1. List the members of the sample space that include a taco. Use parentheses.

   _____

2. List the members of the sample space that include cheese. Use parentheses.

   _____

3. What is the probability of choosing a burrito with cheese and a taco or a wrap with salsa? Explain.

   _____

   _____

Use the information below to answer questions 4–6.

A basket of 40 pairs of pliers at a discount hardware store includes 5 pairs of 6-inch pliers. A second basket contains 20 hammers, including 3 large hammers.

4. What is the probability of drawing a 6-inch pair of pliers from the first

   basket without looking?_____

5. What is the probability of **not** drawing a large hammer from the second

   basket without looking?_____

6. What is the probability of drawing a pair of 6-inch pliers and

   not drawing a large hammer?_____

7. What is the probability of drawing a pair of 6-inch pliers from the

   second basket? Explain. _____

LESSON 13-2

Theoretical Probability of Compound Events

Reteach

Compound probability is the likelihood of two or more events occurring.

1. To identify the sample space, use a list, tree diagram, or table. If order does not matter, cross out repeated combinations that differ only by order.

2. Count the number of outcomes in the desired event.

3. Divide by the total number of possible outcomes.

A student spins the spinner and rolls a number cube What is the probability that she will randomly spin a 1 and roll a number less than 4?

1. Identify the sample space.

2. Count the number of desired outcomes: 3.

3. Divide by the total number possibilities: 18.

$$\text{Probability (1 and} < 4) = \frac{3}{18} = \frac{1}{6}$$

	1	2	3	4	5	6
1	1-1	1-2	1-3	1-4	1-5	1-6
2	2-1	2-2	2-3	2-4	2-5	2-6
3	3-1	3-2	3-3	3-4	3-5	3-6

At a party, sandwiches are served on 5 types of bread: multi-grain, pita, rye, sourdough, and whole wheat. Sam and Ellen each randomly grab a sandwich. What is the probability that Ellen gets a sandwich on pita or rye and Sam gets a sandwich on multi-grain or sourdough?

1. The table shows the sample space. Draw an X in each cell in which Ellen gets a sandwich on pita or rye.

2. Draw a circle in each cell in which Sam gets a sandwich on multi-grain or sourdough.

3. Count the number of possibilities that have both an oval and a rectangle.

_____

4. Divide the number you counted in Step 4 by the total number of possibilities in the sample space.

_____

This is the probability that Ellen gets a pita or a rye sandwich *and* that Sam gets a multi-grain or a sourdough sandwich.

		Ellen				
		M	P	R	S	W
Sam	M					
	P					
	R					
	S					
	W					

Making Predictions with Theoretical Probability
Practice and Problem Solving: A/B

In each odd-numbered question, find the theoretical probability. Then use that probability to make a prediction in the even-numbered question that follows it.

1. Martin flips a coin. What is the probability that the coin will land on heads?

   _____

2. Martin flips the coin 64 times. How many times can Martin expect the coin to land on heads?

   _____

3. A spinner is divided into five equal sections labeled 1 to 5. What is the probability that the spinner will land on 3?

   _____

4. If the spinner is spun 60 times, how many times can you expect the spinner to land on 3?

   _____

5. Harriet rolls a number cube. What is the probability that the number cube will land on 3 or 4?

   _____

6. If Harriet rolls the number cube 39 times, how many times can she expect to roll a 3 or 4?

   _____

7. A bag contains 6 red and 10 black marbles. If you pick a marble from the bag, what is the probability that the marble will be black?

   _____

8. If you pick a marble, record its color, and return it to the bag 200 times, how many times can you expect to pick a black marble?

   _____

Make a prediction based on the theoretical probability.

9. Gill rolls a number cube 78 times. How many times can he expect to roll an odd number greater than 1?

   _____

10. Jenna flips two pennies 105 times. How many times can she expect both coins to come up heads?

    _____

11. A shoebox holds a number of disks of the same size. There are 5 red, 6 white, and 7 blue disks. You pick out a disk, record its color, and return it to the box. If you repeat this process 250 times, how many times can you expect to pick either a red or white disk?

    _____

12. Ron draws 16 cards from a deck of 52 cards. The deck is made up of cards of four different colors—red, blue, yellow, and green. How many of the cards drawn can Ron expect to be green?

    _____

Making Predictions with Theoretical Probability

LESSON 13-3

Reteach

Predictions are thoughtful guesses about what will happen.
You can create an "outcome tree" to keep track of outcomes.

Sally is going to roll a number cube 21 times.
She wants to know how many times she can expect to roll a 1 or 4.

There are a total of 6 **outcomes**.
Of these, *two* outcomes (1 and 4) are desirable.

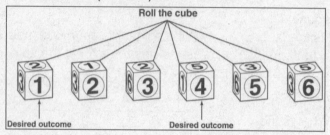

Use probability to predict the number of times Sally would roll a 1 or 4.

$$P(1\,or\,4) = \frac{\text{number of desirable outcomes}}{\text{number of possible outcomes}} = \frac{2}{6} = \frac{1}{3}$$

Set up a proportion relating the probability to the number of tries.

$$\frac{1}{3} = \frac{x}{21}$$

$3x = 21$ Cross-multiply.

$x = 7$ Simplify.

In 21 tries, Sally can expect to roll seven 1s or 4s.

**For each odd-numbered question, find the theoretical probability.
Use that probability to make a prediction in the even-numbered
question that follows it.**

1. Sandra flips a coin. What is the probability that the coin will land on tails?

_____

2. Sandra flips the coin 20 times. How many times can Sandra expect the coin to land on tails?

_____

3. A spinner is divided into four equal sections labeled 1 to 4. What is the probability that the spinner will land on 2?

_____

4. If the spinner is spun 80 times, how often can you expect it to land on 2?

_____

Using Technology to Conduct a Simulation

LESSON 13-4

Practice and Problem Solving: A/B

Answer the questions below.

1. A marine biologist has historical records to show that the chance of finding shrimp in a catch of ocean animals is 20 percent. The simulation below models the experimental probability of finding shrimp in at least one of the next 5 catches. The numbers 1 and 2 represent catches with shrimp. The numbers 3–10 represent catches without shrimp.

    a. What does the marine biologist do?

    _____

    _____

    b. Here is the table the marine biologist created. Fill in the missing data.

Trial	Numbers Generated	Shrimp Caught	Trial	Numbers Generated	Shrimp Caught
1	7, 3, 2, 7, 10		6	8, 4, 7, 6, 5	
2	2, 4, 5, 3, 10		7	6, 10, 1, 7, 6	
3	9, 9, 7, 6, 6		8	7, 9, 8, 3, 8	
4	7, 9, 6, 6, 4		9	1, 4, 4, 8, 9	
5	10, 6, 4, 6, 4		10	7, 8, 9, 5, 3	

2. According to the simulation above, what is the experimental probability that shrimp will be caught in at least one of the next 5 catches?

    _____

3. At a television game show, prizes are placed under 10 percent of the seats in the studio audience. What is the experimental probability that you have to reserve exactly 4 seats before you win a prize?

    a. Describe a model to use for this simulation.

    _____

    _____

    _____

    b. Give an example of a trial that would result in winning a prize for exactly 4 seats.

    _____

LESSON 13-4

Using Technology to Conduct a Simulation
Reteach

Use a graphing calculator to help you conduct a probability simulation.

There is a 20 percent possibility of rain during the week of the school fair. What is the experimental probability that it will rain on at least one of the days of the festival, Monday through Friday?

Step 1 Choose a model.

Probability of rain: $20\% = \dfrac{20}{100} = \dfrac{1}{5}$

Use whole numbers 1–5 for the days.
  Rain: 1   No rain: 2–5

Step 2 Generate random numbers from 1 to 5 until you get a 1.

Example: 1, 2, 2, 5, 2
This trial counts as an outcome that it will rain on at least one of the days of a week.

Step 3 Perform multiple trials by repeating Step 2:

Trial	Numbers Generated	Rain	Trial	Numbers Generated	Rain
1	1, 2, 2, 5, 2	1	6	1, 4, 5, 5, 3	1
2	5, 2, 2, 2, 3	0	7	3, 4, 5, 2, 2	0
3	5, 2, 3, 1, 5	1	8	4, 1, 2, 2, 2	1
4	3, 2, 3, 2, 2	0	9	2, 2, 2, 4, 2	0
5	3, 2, 2, 2, 2	0	10	2, 2, 4, 3, 3	0

Step 4 In 10 trials, the experimental probability that it will rain on 1 of the

school days is 4 out of 10 or 40 percent, 0.4, or $\dfrac{2}{5}$ (two-fifths).

Find the experimental probability. Draw a table on a separate sheet of paper and use 10 trials.

1. An event has 5 outcomes. Each outcome: 50-50 chance or more.

_____

_____

2. An event has a 40 percent probability. Each outcome: exactly 3-in-5 chance.

_____

_____

LESSON 14-1

Rational and Irrational Numbers

Practice and Problem Solving: A/B

Write each fraction as a decimal.

1. $\dfrac{1}{8}$

2. $\dfrac{9}{16}$

3. $\dfrac{11}{20}$

4. $5\dfrac{8}{25}$

_____

5. $\dfrac{14}{15}$

6. $2\dfrac{7}{12}$

7. $\dfrac{3}{100}$

8. $\dfrac{16}{5}$

_____

Find the two square roots of each number.

9. 25

10. 1

11. $\dfrac{25}{4}$

12. $\dfrac{121}{49}$

_____

Find the cube root of each number.

13. 8

14. 216

15. 1

16. 2197

_____

Approximate each irrational number to the nearest hundredth without using a calculator.

17. $\sqrt{32}$

18. $\sqrt{118}$

19. $\sqrt{18}$

20. $\sqrt{319}$

_____

Approximate each irrational number to the nearest hundredth without using a calculator. Then plot each number on a number line.

21. $\sqrt{8}$ _____

22. $\sqrt{75}$ _____

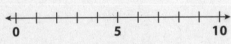

23. A tablet weighs 1.23 pounds. What is its weight written as a mixed number?

_____

24. The area of a square mirror is 256 in². A rectangular mirror has a width the same as the square mirror's width. Its length is two inches longer than its width. What is the area of the rectangular mirror?

_____

LESSON 14-1

Rational and Irrational Numbers
Reteach

To write a fraction as a decimal, divide the numerator by the denominator.

A decimal may terminate.

$$\frac{3}{4} = 4\overline{)3.00}$$
$$\phantom{\frac{3}{4} = 4} \quad 0.75$$
$$\phantom{\frac{3}{4} = 4)} \underline{-28\downarrow}$$
$$\phantom{\frac{3}{4} = 4)} \quad 20$$
$$\phantom{\frac{3}{4} = 4)} \underline{-20}$$
$$\phantom{\frac{3}{4} = 4)} \quad \ \ 0$$

A decimal may repeat.

$$\frac{1}{3} = 3\overline{)1.00}$$
$$\phantom{\frac{1}{3} = 3} \quad 0.\overline{3}$$
$$\phantom{\frac{1}{3} = 3)} \underline{-9\downarrow}$$
$$\phantom{\frac{1}{3} = 3)} \quad 10$$
$$\phantom{\frac{1}{3} = 3)} \underline{-\ 9}$$
$$\phantom{\frac{1}{3} = 3)} \quad \ \ 1$$

Complete to write each fraction as a decimal.

1. $\dfrac{15}{4} = 4\overline{)15.00}$

2. $\dfrac{5}{6} = 6\overline{)5.00}$

3. $\dfrac{11}{3} = 3\overline{)11.00}$

Every positive number has two square roots, one positive and one negative.

Since $5 \times 5 = 25$ and also $-5 \times -5 = 25$, both 5 and -5 are square roots of 25.

$\sqrt{25} = 5$ and $-\sqrt{25} = -5$

Every positive number has one cube root.
Since $4 \times 4 \times 4 = 64$, 4 is the cube root of 64.

Find the two square roots for each number.

4. 81

5. 49

6. $\dfrac{25}{36}$

_____ _____ _____

Find the cube root for each number.

7. 27

8. 125

9. 729

_____ _____ _____

Name _____ Date _____ Class_____

Sets of Real Numbers

Practice and Problem Solving: A/B

List all number sets that apply to each number.

1. $-\dfrac{4}{5}$

_____

2. $\sqrt{15}$

_____

3. -2

_____

4. -25

_____

5. $0.\overline{3}$

_____

6. $\dfrac{20}{4}$

_____

Tell whether the given statement is true or false. Explain your choice.

7. All real numbers are rational.

_____

8. All whole numbers are integers.

_____

**Identify the set of numbers that best describes each situation.
Explain your choice.**

9. the amount of money in a bank account

_____

10. the exact temperature of a glass of water in degrees Celsius

_____

Place each number in the correct location on the Venn diagram.

11. $-\dfrac{5}{9}$

12. $-\sqrt{100}$

13. π

14. $\sqrt{25}$

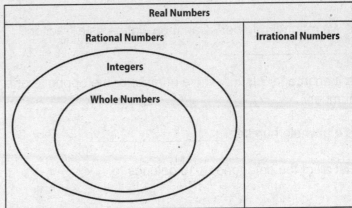

Sets of Real Numbers

LESSON 14-2

Reteach

Numbers can be organized into groups. Each number can be placed into one or more of the groups.

Real numbers include all rational and irrational numbers. All of the numbers that we use in everyday life are real numbers.

- If a real number can be written as a fraction, it is a **rational number**. If it cannot be written as a fraction, it is an **irrational number**.

- If a rational number is a whole number, or the opposite of a whole number, then it is an **integer**.

- If an integer is positive or 0, then it is a **whole number**.

You can use these facts to categorize any number.

A. What kind of number is 10?

Is it a real number? *Yes.*

Is it a rational number? Can it be written as a fraction? *Yes:* $\frac{10}{1}$

Is it an integer? Is it a whole number or the opposite of a whole number? *Yes.*

Is it a whole number? *Yes.*

So 10 is a real number, a rational number, an integer, and a whole number.

B. What kind of number is $\sqrt{\frac{9}{3}}$?

Is it a real number? *Yes.*

Is it a rational number? Can it be written as a fraction? *No.* $\frac{9}{3}$ *simplifies to 3. If you try to find the square root of 3, you will get a decimal answer that goes on forever but does not repeat: 1.7320508… This cannot be written as a fraction.*

So $\sqrt{\frac{9}{3}}$ is a real, irrational number.

Answer each question to identify the categories the given number belongs to.

$\sqrt{16}$

1. Is it a real number? _____

2. Is it a rational number? Can it be written as a fraction?

   _____

3. Is it an integer? Is it a whole number or the opposite of a whole number? _____

4. Is it a whole number? _____

5. List all of the categories $\sqrt{16}$ belongs to.

   _____

LESSON 14-3

Ordering Real Numbers

Practice and Problem Solving: A/B

Compare. Write <, >, or = .

1. $\sqrt{5} + 3 \bigcirc \sqrt{5} + 4$

2. $\sqrt{6} + 13 \bigcirc \sqrt{10} + 13$

3. $\sqrt{7} + 4 \bigcirc 5 + \sqrt{6}$

4. $8 + \sqrt{2} \bigcirc \sqrt{8} + 2$

5. $3 + \sqrt{3} \bigcirc \sqrt{13} - 7$

6. $11 - \sqrt{3} \bigcirc 5 - \sqrt{3}$

Use the table to answer the questions.

7. List the butterflies in order from greatest to least wingspan.

   _____

   _____

   _____

   _____

Butterfly	Wingspan (in.)
Great white	3.75
Large orange sulphur	$3\frac{3}{8}$
Apricot sulphur	2.625
White-angled sulphur	3.5

8. The pink-spotted swallowtail's wingspan can measure $3\frac{5}{16}$ inches.

   Between which two butterflies should the pink-spotted swallowtail be in your list from question 7?

   _____

Order each group of numbers from least to greatest.

9. $\sqrt{8}$, 2, $\frac{\sqrt{7}}{2}$

10. $\sqrt{12}$, π, 3.5

   _____

   _____

11. $\sqrt{26}$, −20, 13.5, $\sqrt{35}$

12. $\sqrt{6}$, −5.25, $\frac{3}{2}$, 5

   _____

   _____

Solve.

13. Four people have used different methods to find the height of a wall. Their results are shown in the table. Order their measurements from greatest to least. $\pi \approx 3.14$

Wall Height (m)			
Allie	**Byron**	**Justin**	**Rosa**
$\sqrt{12} - 1$	$\frac{5}{2}$	2.25	$1 + \frac{\pi}{2}$

   _____

LESSON
14-3

Ordering Real Numbers
Reteach

Compare and order real numbers from least to greatest.

Order $\sqrt{22}$, $\pi + 1$, and $4\frac{1}{2}$ from least to greatest.

You can use a calculator to approximate irrational numbers.

$\sqrt{22} \approx 4.69$

You know that $\pi \approx 3.14$, so you can find the approximate value of $\pi + 1$.

$\pi + 1 \approx 3.14 + 1 \approx 4.14$

Plot $\sqrt{22}$, $\pi + 1$, and $4\frac{1}{2}$ on a number line.

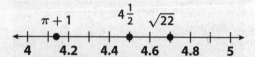

On a number line, the values of numbers increase as you move from left to right. So, to order these numbers from least to greatest, list them from left to right.

$\pi + 1$, $4\frac{1}{2}$, and $\sqrt{22}$

Order each group of numbers from least to greatest.

1. 4, π, $\sqrt{8}$

_____

2. 5, $\dfrac{17}{3}$, $\pi + 2$

_____

3. $\sqrt{2}$, 1.7, -2

_____

4. 2.5, $\sqrt{5}$, $\dfrac{3}{2}$

_____

5. 3.7, $\sqrt{13}$, $\pi + 1$

_____

6. $\dfrac{5}{4}$, $\pi - 2$, $\dfrac{\sqrt{5}}{2}$

_____

Integer Exponents

LESSON
15-1

Practice and Problem Solving: A/B

Find the value of each power.

1. $5^3 =$ _____

2. $7^{-2} =$ _____

3. $51^1 =$ _____

4. $3^{-4} =$ _____

5. $1^{12} =$ _____

6. $64^0 =$ _____

7. $4^{-3} =$ _____

8. $4^3 =$ _____

9. $10^5 =$ _____

Find the missing exponent.

10. $n^3 = n^{\boxed{}} \bullet n^{-3}$

11. $\dfrac{a^{\boxed{}}}{a^2} = a^4$

12. $(r^4)^{\boxed{}} = r^{12}$

Simplify each expression.

13. $(9 - 3)^2 - (5 \bullet 4)^0 =$ _____

14. $(2 + 3)^5 \div (5^2)^2 =$ _____

15. $4^2 \div (6 - 2)^4 =$ _____

16. $[(1 + 7)^2]^2 \bullet (12^2)^0 =$ _____

Use the description below to complete Exercises 17–20.

A shipping company makes a display to show how many cubes can fit into a large box. Each cube has sides of 2 inches. The large box has sides of 10 inches.

17. Use exponents to express the volume of each cube and the large box.

Volume of cube = _____   Volume of large box = _____

18. Find how many cubes will fit in the box. _____

19. Suppose the shipping company were packing balls with a diameter of 2 inches instead of cubes. Would the large box hold more balls or fewer balls than boxes? Explain your answer.

_____

_____

_____

20. Suppose the size of each cube is doubled and the size of the large box is doubled. How many of these new cubes will fit in that new large box? Explain how you found your answer.

_____

_____

LESSON 15-1

Integer Exponents
Reteach

A positive exponent tells you how many times to multiply the base as a factor. A negative exponent tells you how many times to divide by the base. Any number to the 0 power is equal to 1.

$$4^2 = 4 \bullet 4 = 16 \qquad 4^5 = 4 \bullet 4 \bullet 4 \bullet 4 \bullet 4 = 1024 \qquad a^3 = a \bullet a \bullet a$$

$$4^{-2} = \frac{1}{4^2} = \frac{1}{4 \bullet 4} = \frac{1}{16} \qquad 4^{-5} = \frac{1}{4^5} = \frac{1}{4 \bullet 4 \bullet 4 \bullet 4 \bullet 4} = \frac{1}{1024} \qquad a^{-3} = \frac{1}{a^3} = \frac{1}{a \bullet a \bullet a}$$

When you work with integers, certain properties are always true. With integer exponents, there are also certain properties that are always true.

When the bases are the same and you multiply, you add exponents.

$$2^2 \bullet 2^4 = 2^{2+4}$$
$$\underbrace{2 \bullet 2} \bullet \underbrace{2 \bullet 2 \bullet 2 \bullet 2} = 2^6 \qquad a^m \bullet a^n = a^{m+n}$$

When the bases are the same and you divide, you subtract exponents.

$$\frac{2^5}{2^3} = 2^{5-3}$$

$$\frac{2 \bullet 2 \bullet \cancel{2} \bullet \cancel{2} \bullet \cancel{2}}{\cancel{2} \bullet \cancel{2} \bullet \cancel{2}} = 2^2 \qquad \frac{a^m}{a^n} = a^{m-n}$$

When you raise a power to a power, you multiply.

$$(2^3)^2 = 2^{3 \bullet 2}$$

$$(2 \bullet 2 \bullet 2)^2 \qquad (a^m)^n = a^{m \bullet n}$$

$$(2 \bullet 2 \bullet 2) \bullet (2 \bullet 2 \bullet 2) = 2^6$$

Tell whether you will add, subtract, or multiply the exponents. Then simplify by finding the value of the expression.

1. $\dfrac{3^6}{3^3} \rightarrow$ _____

2. $8^2 \bullet 8^{-3} \rightarrow$ _____

3. $(3^2)^3 \rightarrow$ _____

4. $5^3 \bullet 5^1 \rightarrow$ _____

5. $\dfrac{4^2}{4^4} \rightarrow$ _____

6. $(6^2)^2 \rightarrow$ _____

Scientific Notation with Positive Powers of 10

LESSON 15-2

Practice and Problem Solving: A/B

Write each number as a power of 10.

1. 100

2. 10,000

3. 100,000

4. 10,000,000

_____

5. 1,000,000

6. 1000

7. 1,000,000,000

8. 1

_____

Write each power of ten in standard notation.

9. 10^3

10. 10^5

11. 10

12. 10^6

_____

13. 10^2

14. 10^0

15. 10^4

16. 10^7

_____

Write each number in scientific notation.

17. 2500

18. 300

19. 47,300

20. 24

_____

21. 14,565

22. 7001

23. 19,050,000

24. 33

_____

Write each number in standard notation.

25. 6×10^3

26. 4.5×10^2

27. 7×10^7

28. 1.05×10^4

_____

29. 3.052×10^3

30. 5×10^0

31. 9.87×10^1

32. 5.43×10^1

_____

Solve.

33. The average distance of the Moon from Earth is about 384,400 kilometers. Write this number in scientific notation.

_____

34. The radius of Earth is about 6.38×10^3 kilometers. Write this distance in standard notation.

_____

LESSON 15-2 Scientific Notation with Positive Powers of 10
Reteach

You can change a number from standard notation to scientific notation in 3 steps.

    1. Place the decimal point between the first and second digits on the left to make a number between 1 and 10.
    2. Count from the decimal point to the right of the last digit on the right.
    3. Use the number of places counted in Step 2 as the power of ten.

Example
Write 125,000 in scientific notation.

1.25   1) The first and second digits to the left are 1 and 2, so place the decimal point between the two digits to make the number 1.25.

125,000

1.25×10^5 2) The last digit in 125,000 is 5 places to the right.
              3) The power of 10 is 5.

You can change a number from scientific notation to standard notation in 3 steps.

    1. Find the power of 10.
    2. Count that number of places to the right.
    3. Add zeros as needed.

Example
Write 5.96×10^4 in standard notation.

10^4 1) The power of 10 is 4.
5.9600

59,600   2) Move the decimal point 4 places to the right.
             3) Add two zeros.

Complete to write each number in scientific notation.

1. 34,600

   The number between 1 and 10: _____

   The power of 10: _____

   The number in scientific notation:

   _____

2. 1,050,200

   The number between 1 and 10: _____

   The power of 10: _____

   The number in scientific notation:

   _____

Write each number in standard notation.

3. 1.057×10^3 4. 3×10^8 5. 5.24×10^5

_____   _____   _____

LESSON 15-3

Scientific Notation with Negative Powers of 10

Practice and Problem Solving: A/B

Write each number as a negative power of ten.

1. $\dfrac{1}{10^2}$ = _____

2. $\dfrac{1}{10^4}$ = _____

3. $\dfrac{1}{10^5}$ = _____

4. $\dfrac{1}{10^7}$ = _____

5. $\dfrac{1}{10^6}$ = _____

6. $\dfrac{1}{10^3}$ = _____

7. $\dfrac{1}{10^9}$ = _____

8. $\dfrac{1}{10^1}$ = _____

Write each power of ten in standard notation.

9. 10^{-3} = _____

10. 10^{-5} = _____

11. 10^{-1} = _____

12. 10^{-6} = _____

13. 10^{-2} = _____

14. 10^{-9} = _____

15. 10^{-4} = _____

16. 10^{-7} = _____

Write each number in scientific notation.

17. 0.025

18. 0.3

19. 0.000473

20. 0.0024

_____

_____

_____

_____

21. 0.000014565

22. 0.70010

23. 0.0190500

24. 0.00330000

_____

_____

_____

_____

Write each number in standard notation.

25. 6×10^{-3}

26. 4.5×10^{-2}

27. 7×10^{-7}

28. 1.05×10^{-6}

_____

_____

_____

_____

29. 3.052×10^{-8}

30. 5×10^{-1}

31. 9.87×10^{-4}

32. 5.43×10^{-5}

_____

_____

_____

_____

Solve.

33. An *E. coli* bacterium has a diameter of about 5×10^{-7} meter. Write this measurement as a decimal in standard notation.

_____

34. A human hair has an average diameter of about 0.000017 meter. Write this measurement in scientific notation.

_____

Scientific Notation with Negative Powers of 10

LESSON 15-3

Reteach

You can convert a number from standard form to scientific notation in 3 steps.

1. Starting from the left, find the first non-zero digit. To the right of this digit is the new location of your decimal point.
2. Count the number of places you moved the decimal point. This number will be used in the exponent in the power of ten.
3. Since the original decimal value was less than 1, your power of ten must be negative. Place a negative sign in front of the exponent.

Example

Write 0.00496 in standard notation.

4.96	1) The first non-zero digit is 4, so move the decimal point to the right of the 4.
4.96×10^3	2) The decimal point moved 3 places, so the whole number in the power of ten is 3.
4.96×10^{-3}	3) Since 0.00496 is less than 1, the power of ten must be negative.

You can convert a number from scientific notation to standard form in 3 steps.

1. Find the power of ten.
2. If the exponent is negative, you must move the decimal point to the left. Move it the number of places indicated by the whole number in the exponent.
3. Insert a leading zero before the decimal point.

Example

Write 1.23×10^{-5} in standard notation.

10^{-5}	1) Find the power of ten.
.0000123	2) The exponent is −5, so move the decimal point 5 places to the left.
0.0000123	3) Insert a leading zero before the decimal point.

Write each number in scientific notation.

1. 0.0279

2. 0.00007100

3. 0.0000005060

_____ _____ _____

Write each number in standard notation.

4. 2.350×10^{-4}

5. 6.5×10^{-3}

6. 7.07×10^{-5}

_____ _____ _____

**LESSON
15-4**

Operations with Scientific Notation
Practice and Problem Solving: A/B

Add or subtract. Write your answer in scientific notation.

1. $6.4 \times 10^3 + 1.4 \times 10^4 + 7.5 \times 10^3$

   _____

2. $4.2 \times 10^6 - 1.2 \times 10^5 - 2.5 \times 10^5$

   _____

3. $3.3 \times 10^9 + 2.6 \times 10^9 + 7.7 \times 10^8$

   _____

4. $8.0 \times 10^4 - 3.4 \times 10^4 - 1.2 \times 10^3$

   _____

Multiply or divide. Write your answer in scientific notation.

5. $(3.2 \times 10^8)(1.3 \times 10^9) = $ _____

6. $\dfrac{8.8 \times 10^7}{4.4 \times 10^4} = $ _____

7. $(1.5 \times 10^6)(5.9 \times 10^4) = $ _____

8. $\dfrac{1.44 \times 10^{10}}{2.4 \times 10^2} = $ _____

Write each number using calculator notation.

9. $4.1 \times 10^4 = $ _____

10. $9.4 \times 10^{-6} = $ _____

Write each number using scientific notation.

11. $5.2E–6 = $ _____

12. $8.3E+2 = $ _____

Use the situation below to complete Exercises 13–16. Express each answer in scientific notation.

A runner tries to keep a consistent stride length in a marathon. But, the length will change during the race. A runner has a stride length of 5 feet for the first half of the race and a stride length of 4.5 feet for the second half.

13. A marathon is 26 miles 385 yards long. That is about 1.4×10^5 feet. How many feet long is half a marathon?

    _____

14. How many strides would it take to finish the first half of the marathon?

    _____

> *Hint*: Write 5 ft as 5.0×10^0 and 4.5 feet as 4.5×10^0.

15. How many strides would it take to finish the second half of the marathon?

    _____

16. How many strides would it take the runner to complete marathon? Express your answer in both scientific notation and standard notation.

    _____

LESSON 15-4 Operations with Scientific Notation
Reteach

To add or subtract numbers written in scientific notation:

Check that the exponents of powers of 10 are the same.
If not, adjust the decimal numbers and the exponents.
Add or subtract the decimal numbers.
Write the sum or difference and the common power of 10 in
  scientific notation format.
Check whether the answer is in scientific notation.
If it is not, adjust the decimal and the exponent.

$(a \times 10^n) + (b \times 10^n) = (a + b) \times 10^n$ $(1.2 \times 10^5) - (9.5 \times 10^4)$
$(a \times 10^n) - (b \times 10^n) = (a - b) \times 10^n$ $(1.2 \times 10^5) - (0.95 \times 10^5)$ ← Adjust to get same
$(1.2 - 0.95) \times 10^5$ exponent.

0.25×10^5 ← Not in scientific notation.

2.5×10^4 ← Answer

To multiply numbers written in scientific notation:

Multiply the decimal numbers.
Add the exponents in the powers of 10.
Check whether the answer is in scientific notation.
If it is not, adjust the decimal numbers and the exponent.

$(a \times 10^n) \times (b \times 10^m) = ab \times 10^{n+m}$ $(2.7 \times 10^8) \times (8.9 \times 10^4)$
$(2.7 \times 8.9) \times 10^{8+4}$

24.03×10^{12} ← Not in scientific notation.

2.403×10^{13} ← Answer

To divide numbers written in scientific notation:

Divide the decimal numbers.
Subtract the exponents in the powers of 10.
Check whether the answer is in scientific notation.
If it is not, adjust the decimal numbers and the exponent.

$(a \times 10^n) \div (b \times 10^m) = a \div b \times 10^{n-m}$ $(6.3 \times 10^7) \div (9.0 \times 10^3)$
$(6.3 \div 9.0) \times 10^{7-3}$

0.7×10^4 ← Not in scientific notation.

7.0×10^3 ← Answer

Compute. Write each answer in scientific notation.

1. $(2.21 \times 10^7) \div (3.4 \times 10^4)$ 2. $(5.8 \times 10^6) - (4.3 \times 10^6)$ 3. $(2.8 \times 10^3)(7.5 \times 10^4)$

_____   _____   _____

Name _____ Date _____ Class _____

Representing Proportional Relationships
Practice and Problem Solving: A/B

Use the table to complete Exercises 1–3.

Feet	1		3	4		6
Inches		24			60	

1. The table shows the relationship between lengths in feet and lengths in inches. Complete the table.

2. Write each pair as a ratio. $\dfrac{\text{inches}}{\text{feet}} \rightarrow \dfrac{}{1} = \dfrac{24}{} = \dfrac{}{3} = \dfrac{}{4} = \dfrac{60}{} = \dfrac{}{6}$

   Each ratio is equal to _____.

3. Let x represent feet. Let y represent inches.

   An equation that describes the relationship is _____.

Use the table to complete Exercises 4 and 5. Tell whether each relationship is proportional. If it is proportional, write an equation that describes the relationship. First define your variables.

Lemonade Recipe

Lemons	1	2	3	4	5	6
Sugar (c)	1.5	3	4.5	6	7.5	9
Water (c)	7	14	21	28	35	42

4. the ratio of lemons to cups of sugar

   _____

5. the ratio of cups of sugar to cups of water

   _____

Use the table to complete Exercise 6.

Distance Traveled Daily on a Family Road Trip

Hours	6	4.5	9	2	3.25	5.75
Distance (mi)	270	229.5	495	60	188.5	281.75

6. Is the relationship shown in the table below proportional? If so, what is the ratio of the hours driven to miles traveled?

   _____

LESSON 16-1
Representing Proportional Relationships
Reteach

A **proportional relationship** is a relationship between two sets of quantities in which the ratio of one quantity to the other quantity is constant. If you divide any number in one group by the corresponding number in the other group, you will always get the same quotient.

> **Example:** Martin mixes a cleaning spray that is 1 part vinegar to 5 parts water.

Proportional relationships can be shown in tables, graphs, or equations.

Table

The table below shows the number of cups of vinegar Martin needs to add to certain amounts of water to mix his cleaning spray.

Martin's Cleaning Spray

Water (c)	5	10	15	20	25
Vinegar (c)	1	2	3	4	5

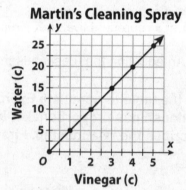
Martin's Cleaning Spray

Notice that if you divide the amount of water by the amount of vinegar, the quotient is always 5.

Graph

On the graph, you can see that for every 1 unit you move to the right on the x-axis, you move up 5 units on the y-axis.

Equation

Let y represent the number of cups of water.
Let x represent the cups of vinegar.

$y = 5x$

Use the table below for Exercises 1–3.

Distance driven (mi)	100	200		400		600
Gas used (gal)	5		15			30

1. There is a proportional relationship between the distance a car drives and the amount of gas used. Complete the table.

2. Find each ratio. $\dfrac{\text{miles}}{\text{gallons}} \rightarrow \dfrac{100}{5} = \dfrac{200}{\rule{1cm}{0.4pt}} = \dfrac{\rule{1cm}{0.4pt}}{15} = \dfrac{400}{\rule{1cm}{0.4pt}} = \dfrac{\rule{1cm}{0.4pt}}{\rule{1cm}{0.4pt}} = \dfrac{600}{30}$

   Each ratio is equal to _____.

3. a. Let x represent gallons of gas used. Let y represent _____.

   b. The equation that describes the relationship is _____.

LESSON 16-2

Rate of Change and Slope
Practice and Problem Solving: A/B

Find the slope of each line.

1. slope = _____

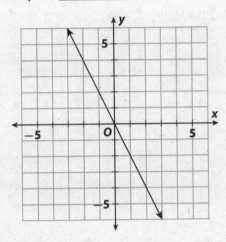

2. slope = _____

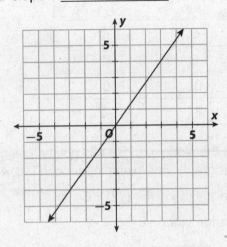

Solve.

3. Jasmine bought 7 yards of fabric. The total cost was $45.43. What was the average cost per yard of the fabric she bought?

_____

4. A train traveled 325 miles in 5 hours. What was the train's average rate of speed in miles per hour?

_____

5. The graph at the right shows the amount of water in a tank that is being filled. What is the average rate of change in gallons per minute?

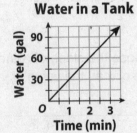

Water in a Tank

_____

6. Suppose the size of the tank in question 5 is doubled. Will the average rate of change in gallons per minute change? Explain your answer.

_____

_____

7. A line passes through (1, 1), (−2, 4), and (6, *n*). Find the value of *n*.

_____

LESSON 16-2 Rate of Change and Slope
Reteach

Look at the relationships between the table, the graph, and the slope.

First value (x)	Second value (y)
–6	4
–3	2
0	0
3	–2

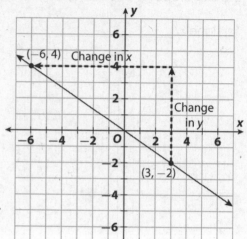

To find the slope, choose two points, using the table or graph. For example, choose (–6, 4) and (3, –2).

Change in y: $4 - (-2) = 6$

Change in x: $-6 - 3 = -9$

Slope $= \dfrac{\text{change in } y}{\text{change in } x} = \dfrac{6}{-9} = -\dfrac{2}{3}$

Use the example above to complete Exercises 1 and 2.

1. The slope is negative. In the table, as the values of x decrease, the

   values of y _____.

2. The slope is negative. In the graph, as you move from left to right, the

   line of the graph is going _____ (up or down).

Solve.

3. Suppose the slope of a line is positive. Describe what happens to the value of x as the value of y increases.

   _____

   _____

4. Suppose the slope of a line is positive. Describe what happens to the graph of the line as you move from left to right.

   _____

   _____

5. Two points on a line are (3, 8) and (–3, 2). What is the slope of the line?

   _____

Name _____ Date _____ Class_____

Interpreting the Unit Rate as Slope

Practice and Problem Solving: A/B

Find the slope. Name the unit rate.

1. **Benjamin Hiking**

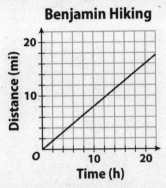

Slope = _____

Unit rate: _____

2. **Marcy Hiking**

Time (h)	5	10	15	20
Distance (mi)	6	12	18	24

Slope =. _____

Unit rate: _____

3. The equation $y = 3.5x$ represents the rate, in miles per hour, at which Laura walks.

   The graph at right represents the rate at which Piyush walks. Determine who walks faster. Explain.

   _____

   _____

Piyush Walking

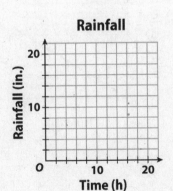

4. Rain fell at a steady rate of 2 inches every 3 hours.

   a. Complete the table to describe the relationship.

Time (h)	3			12
Rainfall (in.)		4	6	

   b. Graph the data in the table on the coordinate grid at right. Draw the line.

   c. Find the slope.

   _____

   d. Identify the unit rate.

   _____

Rainfall

Name _____ Date _____ Class_____

Interpreting the Unit Rate as Slope
Reteach

A rate is a comparison of two quantities that have different units.

A **unit rate** is a rate in which the second quantity is 1 unit.

For example, walking 10 miles every *5 hours* is a rate. Walking 2 miles every *1 hour* is the equivalent unit rate.

$$\frac{10 \text{ miles}}{5 \text{ hours}} = \frac{2 \text{ miles}}{1 \text{ hour}} = 2 \text{ mi/h}$$

The slope of a graph represents the unit rate. To find the unit rate, find the slope.

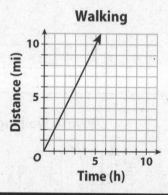

Walking

Step 1: Use the origin and another point to find the slope.

$$\text{slope} = \frac{\text{rise}}{\text{run}} = \frac{10 - 0}{5 - 0} = \frac{10}{5} = 2$$

Step 2: Write the slope as the unit rate.

$$\text{slope} = \text{unit rate} = 2 \text{ mi/h}$$

Find the slope of the graph and the unit rate.

1. **Scott Hiking**

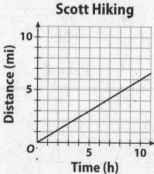

$$\text{slope} = \frac{\text{rise}}{\text{run}} = \underline{\hspace{2cm}}$$

unit rate = _____ mi/h

2. **Rebecca Hiking**

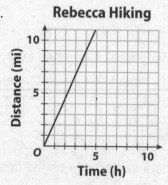

$$\text{slope} = \frac{\text{rise}}{\text{run}} = \underline{\hspace{2cm}}$$

unit rate = _____ mi/h

Name _____ Date _____ Class _____

Representing Linear Nonproportional Relationships

Practice and Problem Solving: A/B

Make a table of values for each equation.

1. $y = 4x + 3$

x	−2	−1	0	1	2
y					

2. $y = \frac{1}{4}x - 2$

x	−8	−4	0	4	8
y					

3. $y = -0.5x + 1$

x	−4	−2	0	2	4
y					

4. $y = 3x + 5$

x	−2	−1	0	1	2
y					

Make a table of values and graph the solutions of each equation.

5. $y = 2x + 1$

x	−2	−1	0	1	2
y					

6. $y = -\frac{1}{2}x - 3$

x	−4	−2	0	2	4
y					

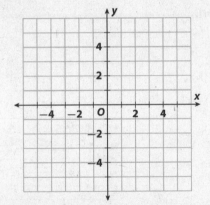

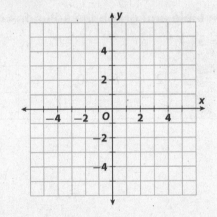

State whether the graph of each linear relationship is a solid line or a set of unconnected points. Explain your reasoning.

7. The relationship between the height of a tree and the time since the tree was planted.

_____

_____

8. The relationship between the number of $12 DVDs you buy and the total cost.

_____

Representing Linear Nonproportional Relationships

LESSON 17-1

Reteach

A relationship will be proportional if the ratios in a table of values of the relationship are constant. The graph of a proportional relationship will be a straight line through the origin. If either of these is not true, the relationship is nonproportional.

To graph the solutions of an equation, make a table of values. Choose values that will give integer solutions.

A. Graph the solutions of $y = x + 2$.

x	−2	−1	0	1	2
y	0	1	2	3	4

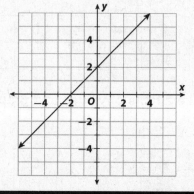

B. Tell whether the relationship is proportional. Explain.

The graph is a straight line, but it does **not** go through the origin, so the relationship is not proportional.

Make a table and graph the solutions of each equation.

1. $y = 3x + 1$

x	−2	−1	0	1	2
y					

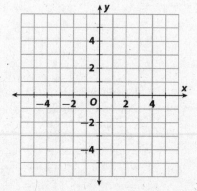

2. $y = -x - 2$

x	−2	−1	0	1	2
y					

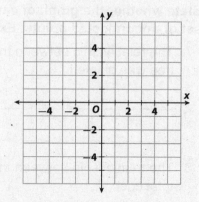

Name _____ Date _____ Class _____

Determining Slope and y-intercept
Practice and Problem Solving: A/B

Find the slope and y-intercept of the line in each graph.

1.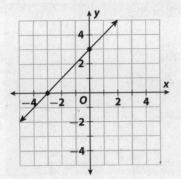

2.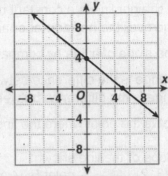

slope m = _____   slope m = _____

y-intercept b = _____   y-intercept b = _____

Find the slope and y-intercept of the line represented by each table.

3.

x	0	3	6	9	12
y		10	19	28	37

4.

x	0	2	4	6	8
y		2	3	4	5

slope m = _____   slope m = _____

y-intercept b = _____   y-intercept b = _____

Find and interpret the rate of change and the initial value.

5. A pizzeria charges $8 for a large cheese pizza, plus $2 for each topping. The total cost for a large pizza is given by the equation $C = 2t + 8$, where t is the number of toppings. Graph the equation for t between 0 and 5 toppings, and explain the meaning of the slope and y-intercept.

_____

_____

_____

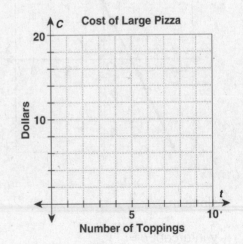

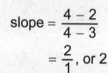

Determining Slope and y-intercept
Reteach

The **slope** of a line is a measure of its tilt, or slant.

The slope of a straight line is a constant ratio, the "rise over run," or the **vertical change** over the **horizontal change**.

You can find the slope of a line by comparing any two of its points.

The vertical change is the difference between the two *y*-values, and the horizontal change is the difference between the two *x*-values.

The **y-intercept** is the point where the line crosses the y-axis.

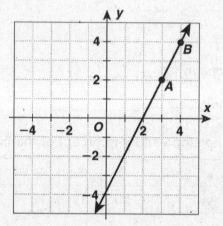

A. Find the slope of the line shown.

point *A*: (3, 2)   point *B*: (4, 4)

$$slope = \frac{4-2}{4-3}$$

$$= \frac{2}{1}, \text{ or } 2$$

So, the slope of the line is 2.

B. Find the *y*-intercept of the line shown.
The line crosses the *y*-axis at (0, –4).
So, the *y*-intercept is –4.

Find the slope and y-intercept of the line in each graph.

1.

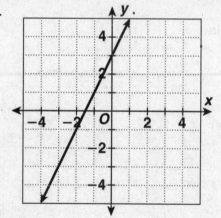

slope *m* = _____

y-intercept *b* = _____

2.

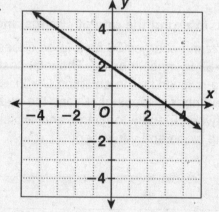

slope *m* = _____

y-intercept *b* = _____

Name _____ Date _____ Class_____

LESSON 17-3

Graphing Linear Nonproportional Relationships Using Slope and y-intercept

Practice and Problem Solving: A/B

Graph each equation using the slope and the *y*-intercept.

1. $y = 2x - 1$

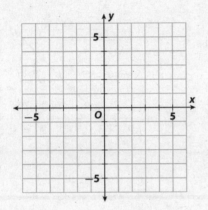

slope = _____ *y*-intercept = _____

2. $y = \frac{1}{2}x + 3$

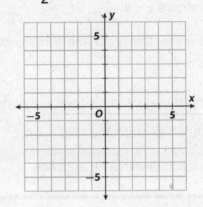

slope = _____ *y*-intercept = _____

3. $y = x - 4$

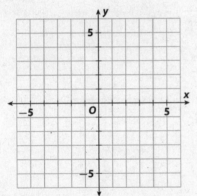

slope = _____ *y*-intercept = _____

4. $y = -x - 2$

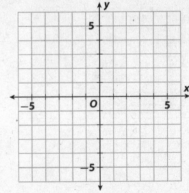

slope = _____ *y*-intercept = _____

5. The equation $y = 15x + 10$ gives your score on a math quiz, where *x* is the number of questions you answered correctly.

   a. Graph the equation.

   b. Interpret the slope and *y*-intercept of the line.

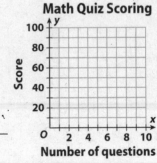

   _____

   _____

   c. What is your score if you answered 5 questions correctly?

   _____

LESSON 17-3

Graphing Linear Nonproportional Relationships Using Slope and *y*-intercept

Reteach

You can graph a linear function by graphing the *y*-intercept of the line and then using the slope to find other points on the line.

The graph shows $y = x + 2$.

To graph the line, first graph the *y*-intercept which is located at (0, 2).

Because the slope is 1 or $\frac{1}{1}$, from the *y*-intercept,

rise 1 and run 1 to graph the next point.

Connect the points with a straight line.

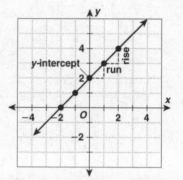

Graph each equation using the slope and the *y*-intercept.

1. $y = 4x - 1$

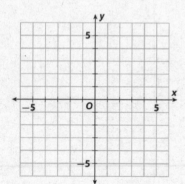

slope = _____ *y*-intercept = _____

2. $y = -\frac{1}{2}x + 2$

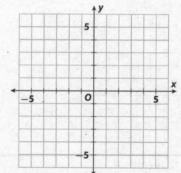

slope = _____ *y*-intercept = _____

3. $y = -x + 1$

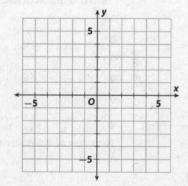

slope = _____ *y*-intercept = _____

4. $y = 2x - 3$

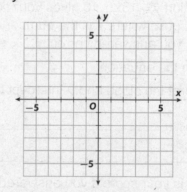

slope = _____ *y*-intercept = _____

Name _____ Date _____ Class _____

LESSON 17-4

Proportional and Nonproportional Situations

Practice and Problem Solving: A/B

Determine if each relationship is a proportional or nonproportional situation. Explain your reasoning. (Assume that the tables represent linear relationships.)

1.
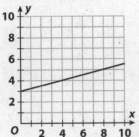

_____

_____

2.
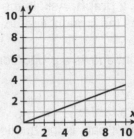

_____

_____

3. $t = 15d$

_____

_____

4. $m = 0.75d - 2$

_____

_____

5. $y = \sqrt{x}$

_____

_____

6. $r = b^2 + 1$

_____

_____

7.

x	y
2	11
5	26
12	61

_____

_____

8.

x	y
4	36
10	90
13	117

_____

_____

LESSON 17-4 Proportional and Nonproportional Situations
Reteach

To decide whether a relationship is proportional or nonproportional, consider how the relationship is presented.

If the relationship is a **graph:** Ask: Is the graph a straight line? Does the straight line go through the origin?
The graph at the right shows a proportional relationship.

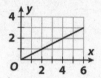

If the relationship is a **table:**
Ask: For every number pair, is the quotient of y and x constant? Will $(0, 0)$ fit the pattern?
The table at the right shows a proportional relationship. The quotient for every number pair is 5. Since each y-value is 5 times each x-value, $(0, 0)$ will fit the pattern.

x	y
4	20
6	30
7	35

If the relationship is an **equation:**
Ask: Is the equation linear? When the equation is written in the form $y = mx + b$ is the value of b equal to 0?
The equation at the right shows a proportional relationship.

$$y = 0.8x$$

Determine if each relationship is a proportional or non-proportional situation. Explain your reasoning.

1.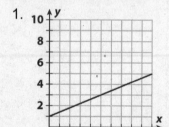

_____

_____

2.

x	y
3	36
5	60
8	96

_____

_____

3. $y = x^3$

_____

_____

4. $q = 4b$

_____

_____

Equations with the Variable on Both Sides
Practice and Problem Solving: A/B

Use algebra tiles to model and solve each equation.

1. $x + 3 = -x - 5$ 2. $1 - 2x = -x - 3$ 3. $x - 2 = -3x + 2$

_____   _____   _____

Fill in the boxes to solve each equation.

4. $4a - 3 = 2a + 7$
    $\underline{-2a \qquad -[\ \ ]}$
    $2a - 3 = 7$
    $\underline{+[\ \ ] \quad +3}$
    $2a = [\ \ ]$
    $\dfrac{2a}{[\ \ ]} = \dfrac{10}{[\ \ ]}$
    $a = [\ \ ]$

5. $7x - 1 = 2x + 5$
    $\underline{-[\ \ ] \qquad -2x}$
    $5x - 1 = [\ \ ]$
    $\underline{+[\ \ ] \qquad +1}$
    $5x = [\ \ ]$
    $\dfrac{5x}{[\ \ ]} = \dfrac{6}{[\ \ ]}$
    $x = \left[\ \ \right]$

6. $-3r + 9 = -4r + 5$
    $\underline{+[\ \ ] \qquad +4r}$
    $r + 9 = 5$
    $\underline{-[\ \ ] \quad -9}$
    $r = [\ \ ]$

Solve.

7. $3y + 1 = 4y - 6$ 8. $2 + 6x = 1 - x$ 9. $5y + 4 = 4y + 5$

_____   _____   _____

Write an equation to represent each relationship. Then solve the equation.

10. Ten less than 3 times a number is the same as the number plus 4.

_____

11. Six times a number plus 4 is the same as the number minus 11.

_____

12. Fifteen more than twice the hours Carla worked last week is the same as three times the hours she worked this week decreased by 15. She worked the same number of hours each week. How many hours did she work each week?

_____

LESSON 18-1

Equations with the Variable on Both Sides
Reteach

If there are variable terms on both sides of an equation, first collect them on one side. Do this by adding or subtracting. When possible, collect the variables on the side of the equation where the coefficient will be positive.

Solve the equation $5x = 2x + 12$.

$$5x = 2x + 12$$
$$\underline{-2x \quad -2x}$$
$$3x = \qquad 12$$
$$\frac{3x}{3} = \frac{12}{3}$$
$$x = 4$$

To collect on left side, subtract $2x$ from both sides of the equation.

Divide by 3.

Check: Substitute into the original equation.

$$5x = 2x + 12$$
$$5(4) \stackrel{?}{=} 2(4) + 12$$
$$20 \stackrel{?}{=} 8 + 12$$
$$20 = 20$$

Solve the equation $-6z + 28 = 9z - 2$.

$$-6z + 28 = 9z - 2$$
$$\underline{+6z \qquad + 6z}$$
$$28 = 15z - 2$$
$$\underline{+2 \qquad +2}$$
$$30 = 15z$$
$$\frac{30}{15} = \frac{15z}{15}$$
$$2 = z$$

To collect on right side, add $6z$ to both sides of the equation.

Add 2 to both sides of the equation.

Divide by 15.

Check: Substitute into the original equation.

$$-6z + 28 = 9z - 2$$
$$-6(2) + 28 \stackrel{?}{=} 9(2) - 2$$
$$-12 + 28 \stackrel{?}{=} 18 - 2$$
$$16 = 16$$

Complete to solve and check each equation.

1. $9m + 2 = 3m - 10$

$$9m + 2 = 3m - 10$$
$$\underline{-[\quad] \qquad -[\quad]}$$
$$6m + 2 = \qquad -10$$
$$\underline{-[\quad] \qquad -[\quad]}$$
$$6m = [\quad]$$
$$\frac{6m}{[\quad]} = \frac{-12}{[\quad]}$$
$$m = [\quad]$$

To collect on left side, subtract ____ from both sides.

Subtract ____ from both sides.

Divide by ____.

Check: Substitute into the original equation.

$$9m + 2 = 3m - 10$$
$$9(\underline{\quad}) + 2 \stackrel{?}{=} 3(\underline{\quad}) - 10$$
$$\underline{\quad} + 2 \stackrel{?}{=} \underline{\quad} - 10$$
$$\underline{\quad} = \underline{\quad}$$

2. $-7d - 22 = 4d$

$$-7d - 22 = 4d$$
$$\underline{+[\quad] \qquad +[\quad]}$$
$$-22 = 11d$$
$$\frac{-22}{[\quad]} = \frac{11d}{[\quad]}$$
$$[\quad] = d$$

To collect on right side, add ____ to both sides.

Divide by ____.

Check: Substitute into the original equation.

$$-7d - 22 = 4d$$
$$-7(\underline{\quad}) - 22 \stackrel{?}{=} 4(\underline{\quad})$$
$$\underline{\quad} - 22 \stackrel{?}{=} \underline{\quad}$$
$$\underline{\quad} = \underline{\quad}$$

LESSON 18-2

Equations with Rational Numbers

Practice and Problem Solving: A/B

Write the least common multiple of the denominators in the equation.

1. $9 + \dfrac{3}{4}x = \dfrac{7}{8}x - 10$ _____

2. $\dfrac{2}{3}x + \dfrac{1}{6} = -\dfrac{3}{4}x + 1$ _____

Describe the operations used to solve the equation.

3. $\dfrac{5}{6}x - 2 = -\dfrac{2}{3}x + 1$

$6\left(\dfrac{5}{6}x - 2\right) = 6\left(-\dfrac{2}{3}x + 1\right)$ _____

$5x - 12 = -4x + 6$ _____

$\dfrac{+4x \qquad +4x}{9x - 12 = \qquad 6}$ _____
_____

$\dfrac{+12 \qquad +12}{9x = 18}$ _____
_____

$\dfrac{9x}{9} = \dfrac{18}{9}$ _____

$x = 2$

Solve.

4. $\dfrac{2}{3}x + \dfrac{1}{3} = \dfrac{1}{3}x + \dfrac{2}{3}$

5. $\dfrac{3}{5}n + \dfrac{9}{10} = -\dfrac{1}{5}n - \dfrac{23}{10}$

6. $\dfrac{5}{6}h - \dfrac{7}{12} = -\dfrac{3}{4}h - \dfrac{13}{6}$

_____   _____   _____

7. $4.5w = 5.1w - 30$

8. $\dfrac{4}{7}y - 2 = \dfrac{3}{7}y + \dfrac{3}{14}$

9. $-0.8a - 8 = 0.2a$

_____   _____   _____

10. Write and solve a real-world problem that can be modeled by the
equation $0.75x - 18.50 = 0.65x$.

_____

_____

_____

_____

LESSON 18-2

Equations with Rational Numbers

Reteach

To solve an equation with a variable on both sides that involves fractions, first get rid of the fractions.

Solve $\frac{3}{4}m + 2 = \frac{2}{3}m + 5$.

$$12\left(\frac{3}{4}m + 2\right) = 12\left(\frac{2}{3}m + 5\right)$$

$$12\left(\frac{3}{4}m\right) + 12(2) = 12\left(\frac{2}{3}m\right) + 12(5)$$

$$9m + 24 = 8m + 60$$

$$\underline{-8m \qquad -8m}$$

$$m + 24 = 60$$

$$\underline{-24 \qquad -24}$$

$$m = 36$$

Multiply both sides of the equation by 12, the LCM of 4 and 3.

Multiply each term by 12.

Simplify.
Subtract 8m from both sides.
Simplify.
Subtract 24 from both sides.
Simplify.

Check: Substitute into the original equation.

$$\frac{3}{4}m + 2 = \frac{2}{3}m + 5$$

$$\frac{3}{4}(36) + 2 \overset{?}{=} \frac{2}{3}(36) + 5$$

$$27 + 2 \overset{?}{=} 24 + 5$$

$$29 = 29$$

Complete to solve and check your answer.

1. $\frac{1}{4}x + 2 = \frac{2}{5}x - 1$

$$[\ \ ]\left(\frac{1}{4}x + 2\right) = [\ \ ]\left(\frac{2}{5}x - 1\right)$$

$$[\ \ ]\left(\frac{1}{4}x\right) + [\ \ ](2) = [\ \ ]\left(\frac{2}{5}x\right) - [\ \ ](1)$$

$$[\ \ ]x + [\ \ ] = [\ \ ]x - [\ \ ]$$

$$\underline{-5x \qquad\qquad -5x}$$

$$40 = 3x - 20$$

$$\underline{+20 \qquad\qquad +20}$$

$$[\ \ ] = 3x$$

$$\frac{60}{[\ \ ]} = \frac{3x}{[\ \ ]}$$

$$[\ \ ] = x$$

Multiply both sides of the equation by ____ the LCM of 4 and 5.

Multiply each term by____.

Simplify.
Subtract ____.
Simplify.
Add____.
Simplify.

Divide both sides by

_____

Simplify.

Check: Substitute into the original equation.

$$\frac{1}{4}x + 2 = \frac{2}{5}x - 1$$

$$\frac{1}{4}(\underline{\ \ }) + 2 \overset{?}{=} \frac{2}{5}(\underline{\ \ }) - 1$$

$$\underline{\ \ } + 2 \overset{?}{=} \underline{\ \ } - 1$$

$$\underline{\ \ } = \underline{\ \ }$$

LESSON 18-3
Equations with the Distributive Property
Practice and Problem Solving: A/B

Solve each equation.

1. $4(x - 2) = x + 10$

2. $\frac{2}{3}(n - 6) = 5n - 43$

_____

_____

3. $-2(y + 12) = y - 9$

4. $8(12 - k) = 3(k + 21)$

_____

_____

5. $8(-1 + m) + 3 = 2\left(m - 5\frac{1}{2}\right)$

6. $2y - 3(2y - 3) + 2 = 31$

_____

_____

Use the situation below to complete Exercises 7–8.

A taxi company charges $2.25 for the first mile and then $0.20 per mile for each additional mile, or $F = \$2.25 + \$0.20(m - 1)$ where F is the fare and m is the number of miles.

7. If Juan's taxi fare was $6.05, how many miles did he travel in the taxi?

_____

8. If Juan's taxi fare was $7.65, how many miles did he travel in the taxi?

_____

Use the situation below to complete Exercises 9–11.

The equation used to estimate typing speed is $S = \frac{1}{5}(w - 10e)$, where S is the accurate typing speed, w is the number of words typed in 5 minutes and e is the number of errors.

9. Ignacio can type 55 words per minute (wpm). In 5 minutes, she types 285 words. How many errors would you expect her to make?

_____

10. If Alexis types 300 words in 5 minutes with 5 errors, what is his typing speed?

_____

11. Johanna receives a report that says her typing speed is 65 words per minute. She knows that she made 4 errors in the 5-minute test. How many words did she type in 5 minutes?

_____

Equations with the Distributive Property

LESSON 18-3

Reteach

When solving an equation, it is important to simplify on both sides of the equal sign before you try to isolate the variable.

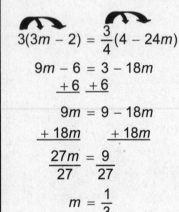

$3(x + 4) + 2 = x + 10$

$3x + 12 + 2 = x + 10$

$3x + 14 = x + 10$
$ \underline{-14 \quad -14}$

$3x = x - 4$
$\underline{-x \quad -x}$

$\dfrac{2x}{2} = \dfrac{-4}{2}$

$x = -2$

Since you cannot combine x and 4, multiply both by 3 using the Distributive Property.
Then combine like terms.

Subtract 14 to begin to isolate the variable term.

Subtract x to get the variables to one side of the equation.

Divide by 2 to isolate the variable.

The solution is -2.

Solve.

1. $5(i + 2) - 9 = -17 - i$

2. $-3(n + 2) = n - 22$

_____

_____

You may need to distribute on both sides of the equal sign before simplifying.

$3(3m - 2) = \dfrac{3}{4}(4 - 24m)$

$9m - 6 = 3 - 18m$
$\underline{+6 \quad +6}$

$9m = 9 - 18m$
$\underline{+18m \qquad +18m}$

$\dfrac{27m}{27} = \dfrac{9}{27}$

$m = \dfrac{1}{3}$

Use the Distributive Property on both sides of the equation to remove the parentheses.

Add 6 to begin to isolate the variable term.

Add $18m$ to get the variables to one side of the equation.

Divide by 27 to isolate the variable.

The solution is $\dfrac{1}{3}$.

Solve.

3. $9(y - 4) = -10\left(y + 2\dfrac{1}{3}\right)$

4. $-7\left(-6 - \dfrac{6}{7}x\right) = 12\left(x - 3\dfrac{1}{2}\right)$

_____

_____

LESSON 18-4 Equations with Many Solutions or No Solution

Practice and Problem Solving: A/B

Tell whether each equation has one, zero, or infinitely many solutions.
If the equation has one solution, solve the equation.

1. $4(x-2) = 4x + 10$

   _____

2. $\frac{1}{2}n + 7 = \frac{n + 14}{2}$

   _____

3. $6(x - 1) = 6x - 1$

   _____

4. $6n + 7 - 2n - 14 = 5n + 1$

   _____

5. $4x + 5 = 9 + 4x$

   _____

6. $\frac{1}{2}(8 - x) = \frac{8 - x}{2}$

   _____

7. $8(y + 4) = 7y + 38$

   _____

8. $4(-8x + 12) = -26 - 32x$

   _____

9. $2(x + 12) = 3x + 24 - x$

   _____

10. $3x - 14 + 2(x - 9) = 2x - 2$

   _____

Solve.

11. Cell phone company A charges $20 per month plus $0.05 per text
    message. Cell phone company B charges $10 per month plus $0.07
    per text message. Is there any number of text messages that will result
    in the exact same charge from both companies?

    _____

12. Lisa's pet shop has 2 fish tanks. Tank A contains smaller fish who are
    fed 1 gram of food each per day. Tank B contains larger fish who are
    fed 2 grams of food each per day. If Tank B contains $\frac{2}{3}$ the number of
    fish that Tank A contains, will Lisa ever feed both tanks the same
    amount of food?

    _____

LESSON 18-4

Equations with Many Solutions or No Solution
Reteach

When you solve a linear equation, you are trying to find a value for the variable that makes the equation true. Often there is only one value that makes an equation true – one solution. But sometimes there is no value that will make the equation true. Other times there are many values that make the equation true.

$x + 3 = 8$

$x = 5$

Use properties of equality to solve.

If you get a statement that tells you what the variable equals, the equation has **one solution**.

$x + 3 = x + 4$

$3 = 4$

If you get a false statement with no variables, the equation has **no solution**.

$x + 3 = x + 3$

$3 = 3$

If you get a true statement with no variables, the equation has infinitely **many solutions**.

Tell whether each equation has one, zero, or infinitely many solutions.

1. $5(i + 2) = 8(i - 1)$

2. $-3(n + 2) = -3n - 6$

_____   _____

You can write an equation with one solution, no solution, or infinitely many solutions.

One solution: Start with a variable on one side and a constant on the other. This is your solution. Add, subtract, multiply or divide both sides of the equation by the same constant(s). Your equation has one solution. **Example:** $3(r + 2) = 30$

No solution: Start with a false statement of equality about two constants, such as $3 = 4$. Now add, subtract, multiply or divide the same variable from both sides. You may then add, subtract, multiply or divide additional constants to both sides. Your equation has no solution. **Example:** $k + 3 = k + 4$

Infinitely many solutions: Start with a true statement of equality about two constants, such as $5 = 5$. Now add, subtract, multiply or divide the same variable from both sides. You may then add, subtract, multiply or divide additional constants to both sides. Your equation has many solutions. **Example:** $5(n - 3) = 5n - 15$

Solve.

3. Write an equation with one solution. _____

4. Write an equation with no solution. _____

5. Write an equation with infinitely many solutions. _____

LESSON 19-1

Properties of Translations

Practice and Problem Solving: A/B

Describe the translation that maps point *A* to point *A'*.

1: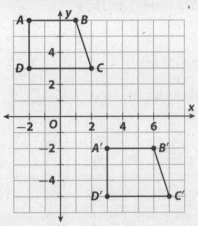

2.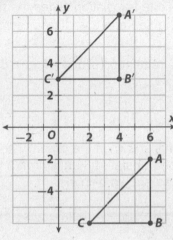

_____   _____

Draw the image of the figure after each translation.

3. 3 units left and 9 units down

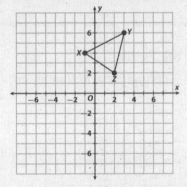

4. 3 units right and 6 units up

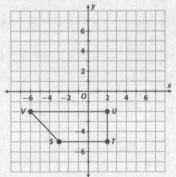

5. a. Graph rectangle *J'K'L'M'*, the image of rectangle *JKLM*, after a translation of 1 unit right and 9 units up.

   b. Find the area of each rectangle.

   _____

   c. Is it possible for the area of a figure to change after it is translated? Explain.

   _____

   _____

Properties of Translations
Reteach

The description of a translation in a coordinate plane uses a combination of two translations – one translation slides the figure in a horizontal direction, and the other slides the figure in a vertical direction. An example is shown below.

A translation slides a figure 8 units right and 5 units down.

horizontal distance   vertical distance

Triangle *LMN* is shown in the graph. The triangle can be translated 8 units right and 5 units down as shown below.

Step 1 Translate each vertex 8 units right.

Step 2 Translate each vertex 5 units down.

Step 3 Label the resulting vertices and connect them to form triangle *L'M'N'*.

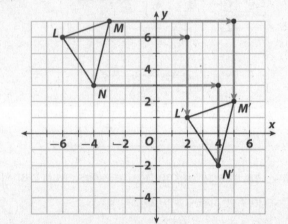

Use a combination of two translations to draw the image of the figure.

1. Translate 6 units left and 7 units down.

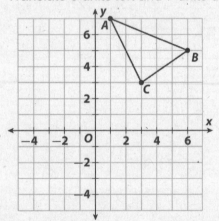

2. Translate 7 units right and 9 units up.

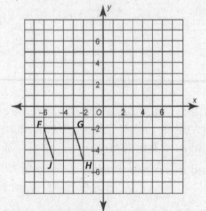

3. When translating a figure using a combination of two translations, is the resulting figure congruent to the original figure? Explain.

_____

_____

LESSON 19-2

Properties of Reflections

Practice and Problem Solving: A/B

Use the graph for Exercises 1–3.

1. Quadrilateral *J* is reflected across the *x*-axis. What is the image of the reflection?

   _____

2. Which two quadrilaterals are reflections of each other across the *y*-axis?

   _____

3. How are quadrilaterals *H* and *J* related?

   _____

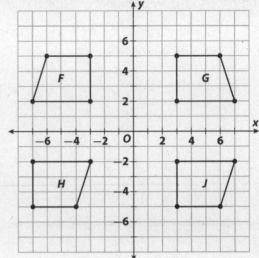

Draw the image of the figure after each reflection.

4. across the *x*-axis

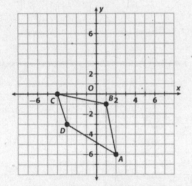

5. across the *y*-axis

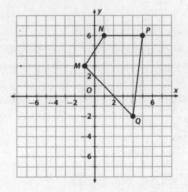

6. a. Graph rectangle *K'L'M'N'*, the image of rectangle *KLMN* after a reflection across the *y*-axis.

   b. What is the perimeter of each rectangle?

   _____

   c. Is it possible for the perimeter of a figure to change after it is reflected? Explain.

   _____

   _____

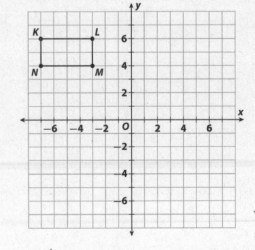

LESSON 19-2

Properties of Reflections
Reteach

You can use tracing paper to reflect a figure in the coordinate plane. The graphs below show how to reflect a triangle across the *y*-axis.

Start by tracing the figure and the axes on tracing paper.

Flip the tracing paper over, making sure to align the axes. Transfer the flipped image onto the coordinate plane.

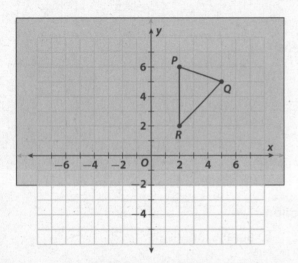
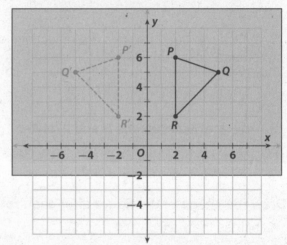

As shown above, flip the paper horizontally for a reflection in the *y*-axis. For a reflection in the *x*-axis, flip the paper vertically.

Use tracing paper to draw the image after the reflection.

1. across the *y*-axis

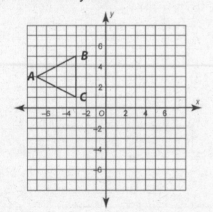

2. across the *x*-axis

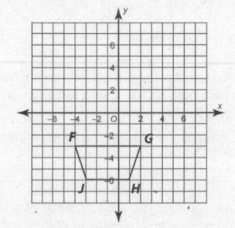

Name _____ Date _____ Class_____

Properties of Rotations
Practice and Problem Solving: A/B

**Use the figures at the right for Exercises 1–5. Triangle
A has been rotated about the origin.**

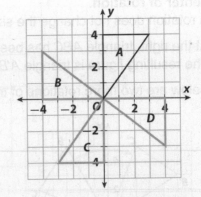

1. Which triangle shows a 90°
   counterclockwise rotation? ____

2. Which triangle shows a 180°
   counterclockwise rotation? ____

3. Which triangle shows a 270°
   clockwise rotation? ____

4. Which triangle shows a 270°
   counterclockwise rotation? ____

5. If the sides of triangle A have lengths of 30 cm,
   40 cm, and 50 cm, what are the lengths of the
   sides of triangle D?

   _____

**Use the figures at the right for Exercises 6–10.
Figure A is to be rotated about the origin.**

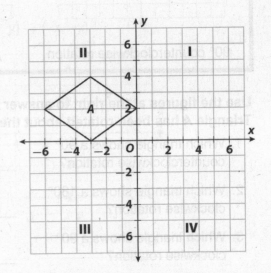

6. If you rotate figure A 90° counterclockwise,
   what quadrant will the image be in? ____

7. If you rotate figure A 270° counterclockwise,
   what quadrant will the image be in? ____

8. If you rotate figure A 180° clockwise,
   what quadrant will the image be in? ____

9. If you rotate figure A 360° clockwise,
   what quadrant will the image be in? ____

10. If the measures of two angles in figure
    A are 60º and 120°, what will the measure
    of those two angles be in the rotated figure?

   _____

Use the grid at the right for Exercises 11–12.

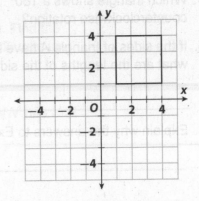

11. Draw a square to show a rotation of 90° clockwise
    about the origin of the given square in quadrant I.

12. What other transformation would result in the same
    image as you drew in Exercise 11?

   _____

LESSON 19-4

Algebraic Representations of Transformations
Reteach

A **transformation** is a change in size or position of a figure. The transformations below change only the position of the figure, not the size.

- A **translation** will *slide* the figure horizontally and/or vertically.
- A **reflection** will *flip* the figure across an axis.
- A **rotation** will *turn* the figure around the origin.

This table shows how the coordinates change with each transformation.

Transformation	Coordinate Mapping
Translation	$(x, y) \rightarrow (x + a, y + b)$ translates left or right a units and up or down b units
Reflection	$(x, y) \rightarrow (-x, y)$ reflects across the y-axis $(x, y) \rightarrow (x, -y)$ reflects across the x-axis
Rotation	$(x, y) \rightarrow (-x, -y)$ rotates 180° around origin $(x, y) \rightarrow (y, -x)$ rotates 90° clockwise around origin $(x, y) \rightarrow (-y, x)$ rotates 90° counterclockwise around origin

A triangle with coordinates of (0, 0), (1, 4), and (3, −2) is transformed so the coordinates are (0, 0), (−4, 1), and (2, 3). What transformation was performed?

Analyze each corresponding pairs of coordinates:

(0, 0) to (0, 0)   Think: Could be reflection or rotation since 0 = −0.

(1, 4) to (−4, 1)   Think: Since x and y are interchanged, it is a rotation and
(3, −2) to (2, 3) y changes sign, so it is a 90° counterclockwise
                                 rotation around origin.

Identify the transformation from the original figure to the image.

1. Original: $A(-2, -4)$, $B(5, 1)$, $C(5, -4)$
   Image: $A'(2, -4)$, $B'(-5, 1)$, $C'(-5, -4)$ _____

2. Original: $A(-8, 2)$, $B(-4, 7)$, $C(-7, 2)$
   Image: $A'(-2, -8)$, $B'(-7, -4)$, $C'(-2, -7)$ _____

3. Original: $A(3, 4)$, $B(-1, 2)$, $C(-3, -5)$
   Image: $A'(3, 8)$, $B'(-1, 6)$, $C'(-3, -1)$ _____

4. Original: $A(1, 1)$, $B(2, -2)$, $C(4, 3)$
   Image: $A'(-1, -1)$, $B'(-2, 2)$, $C'(-4, -3)$ _____

5. Original: $A(-5, -6)$, $B(-2, 4)$, $C(3, 0)$
   Image: $A'(-5, 6)$, $B'(-2, -4)$, $C'(3, 0)$ _____

Name _____ Date _____ Class_____

LESSON 19-5 **Congruent Figures**

Practice and Problem Solving: A/B

Identify a sequence of transformations that will transform figure A into figure C.

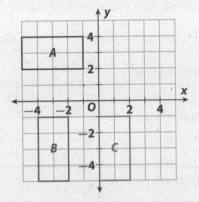

1. What transformation is used to transform figure A to figure B?

_____

2. What transformation is used to transform figure B to figure C?

_____

3. What sequence of transformations is used to transform figure A to figure C? Express the transformations algebraically.

_____

Complete each transformation.

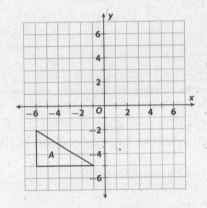

4. Transform figure A by reflecting it over the y-axis. Label the new figure, B.

5. Transform figure B to figure C by applying $(x, y) \rightarrow (x, y + 5)$.

6. Transform figure C to figure D by rotating it 90° counterclockwise around the origin.

7. Compare figure A with figure D. Are the two figures congruent? _____

8. Do figures A and D have the same or different orientation? _____

Alice wanted a pool in location A on the map at the right. However, underground wires forced her to move the pool to location B.

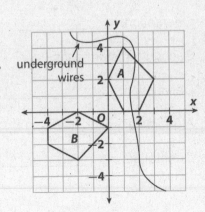

9. What transformations were applied to the pool at location A to move it to location B?

_____

_____

10. Did the relocation change the size or orientation of the pool?

_____

Congruent Figures

Reteach

When combining the transformations below, the original figure and transformed figure are **congruent**. Even though the size does not change, the orientation of the figure might change.

Transformation	Algebraic Coordinate Mapping	Orientation
Translation	$(x, y) \rightarrow (x + a, y + b)$ translates left or right a units and up or down b units	same
Reflection	$(x, y) \rightarrow (-x, y)$ reflects across the y-axis $(x, y) \rightarrow (x, -y)$ reflects across the x-axis	different
Rotation	$(x, y) \rightarrow (-x, -y)$ rotates 180° around origin $(x, y) \rightarrow (y, -x)$ rotates 90° clockwise around origin $(x, y) \rightarrow (-y, x)$ rotates 90° counterclockwise around origin	different

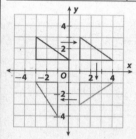

1st transformation: translation right 4 units
$(x, y) \rightarrow (x + 4, y)$, orientation: same

2nd transformation: reflection over the x-axis
$(x, y) \rightarrow (x, -y)$, orientation: different

3rd transformation: rotation 90° clockwise
$(x, y) \rightarrow (y, -x)$ orientation: different

Describe each transformation. Express each algebraically.
Tell whether the orientation is the same or different.

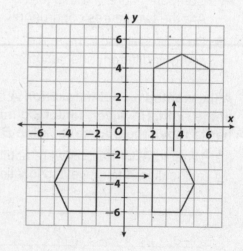

1. First transformation

   Description: _____

   Algebraically: _____

   Orientation: _____

2. Second transformation

   Description: _____

   Algebraically: _____

   Orientation: _____

LESSON 20-1
Properties of Dilations

Practice and Problem Solving: A/B

Use triangles *ABC* and *A'B'C'* for Exercises 1–4.

1. Use the coordinates to find the lengths of the sides.

   Triangle *ABC*: *AB* = ____ ; *BC* = ____

   Triangle *A'B'C'*: *A'B'* = ____ ; *B'C'* = ____

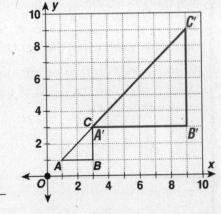

2. Find the ratios of the corresponding sides.

   $\dfrac{A'B'}{AB}$ = ——— = ——— $\qquad$ $\dfrac{B'C'}{BC}$ = ——— = ———

3. Is triangle *A'B'C'* a dilation of triangle *ABC*? _____

4. If triangle *A'B'C'* is a dilation of triangle
   ABC, is it a reduction or an enlargement? _____

For Exercises 5–8, tell whether one figure is a dilation of the other or not. If one figure is a dilation of the other, tell whether it is an enlargement or a reduction. Explain your reasoning.

5. Triangle *R'S'T'* has sides of 3 cm, 4 cm, and 5 cm. Triangle *RST* has sides of 12 cm, 16 cm, and 25 cm.

   _____

   _____

6. Quadrilateral *WBCD* has coordinates of *W*(0, 0), *B*(0, 4), *C*(–6, 4), and *D*(–6, 0). Quadrilateral *W'B'C'D'* has coordinates of *W'*(0, 0), *B'*(0, 2), *C'*(–3, 2), and *D'*(–3, 0).

   _____

   _____

7. Triangle *MLQ* has sides of 4 cm, 4 cm, and 7 cm. Triangle *M'L'Q'* has sides of 12 cm, 12 cm, and 21 cm.

   _____

   _____

8. Do the figures at the right show a dilation? Explain.

   _____

   _____

   _____

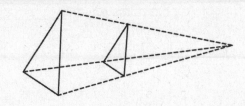

LESSON 20-1
Properties of Dilations
Reteach

A **dilation** can change the size of a figure without changing its shape.

Lines drawn through the corresponding vertices meet at a point called the **center of dilation**.

To determine whether a transformation is a dilation, compare the ratios of the lengths of the corresponding sides.

$$\frac{A'B'}{AB} = \frac{2}{1} = 2$$

$$\frac{B'C'}{BC} = \frac{6}{3} = 2$$

The ratios are equal, so the triangles are similar, and the transformation is a dilation.

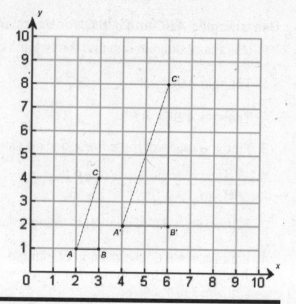

Determine whether each transformation is a dilation.

1.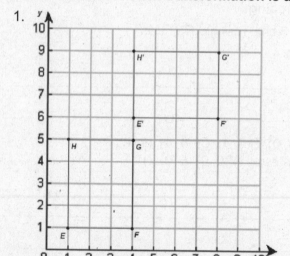

$$\frac{E'F'}{EF} = \frac{\quad}{\quad} = \underline{\quad}$$

$$\frac{F'G'}{FG} = \frac{\quad}{\quad} = \underline{\quad}$$

Are the ratios equal?_____

Is this a dilation?_____

2.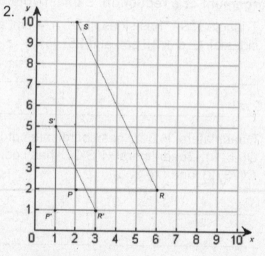

$$\frac{P'R'}{PR} = \frac{\quad}{\quad} = \underline{\quad}$$

$$\frac{P'S'}{PS} = \frac{\quad}{\quad} = \underline{\quad}$$

Are the ratios equal?_____

Is this a dilation?_____

LESSON 20-3

Similar Figures

Practice and Problem Solving: A/B

Identify a sequence of transformations that will transform figure A into figure C. Express each transformation algebraically.

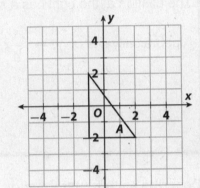

— Figure A

— Figure B

-- Figure C

1. What transformation is used to transform figure A to figure B?

   _____

2. What transformation is used to transform figure B to figure C?

   _____

3. Name two figures that are congruent. _____

4. Name two figures that are similar, but not congruent. _____

Complete each transformation.

5. Transform figure A to figure B by applying $(x, y) \rightarrow (2x, 2y)$.

6. Transform figure B to figure C by rotating it 90° clockwise around the origin.

7. Name two figures that are congruent.

   _____

8. Name two figures that are similar, but not congruent.

   _____

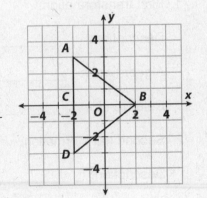

Geraldo designed a flag for his school. He started with △ABC. He used centimeter grid paper. To create the actual flag, the drawing must be dilated using a scale factor of 50. Express each transformation algebraically.

9. What transformation was used to create △CBD from △ABC?

   _____

10. How long will each side of the actual flag ABD be?

    _____

11. The principal decides he wants the flag to hang vertically with side AD on top. What transformation should Geraldo use on △ABD on his drawing so it is in the desired orientation?

    _____

LESSON
20-3

Similar Figures
Reteach

Multiple dilations can be applied to a figure. If one of the transformations is a **dilation**, the figure and its image are **similar**. The size of the figure is changed but the shape is not.

In a dilation, when the scale is a greater than 1, the image is an **enlargement**. When the scale is a fraction between 0 and 1, the image is a **reduction**.

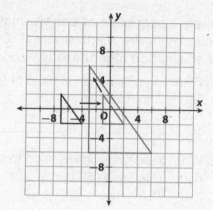

1st transformation: translation right 6 units
                        $(x, y) \rightarrow (x + 6, y)$,
                        relative size: congruent

2nd transformation: dilation by a scale of 3
                        $(x, y) \rightarrow (3x, 3y)$
                        relative size: similar

The dilation at the right has a scale of $\frac{1}{4}$.

Algebraically it is $(x, y) \rightarrow \left(\frac{1}{4}x, \frac{1}{4}y\right)$

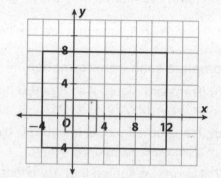

Describe each transformation. Express each one algebraically. Tell whether the figure and its image are congruent or are similar.

1. First transformation:

   Description: _____

   Algebraically: _____

   Relative size: _____

2. Second transformation:

   Description: _____

   Algebraically: _____

   Relative size: _____

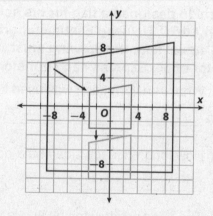

LESSON 21-1

Parallel Lines Cut by a Transversal

Practice and Problem Solving: A/B

Use the figure at the right for Exercises 1–6.

1. Name both pairs of alternate interior angles.

   _____

2. Name the corresponding angle to ∠3. _____

3. Name the relationship between ∠1 and ∠5.

   _____

4. Name the relationship between ∠2 and ∠3.

   _____

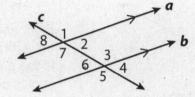

5. Name an interior angle that is supplementary to ∠7. _____

6. Name an exterior angle that is supplementary to ∠5. _____

Use the figure at the right for problems 7–10. Line MP ∥ line QS. Find the angle measures.

7. m∠KRQ when m∠KNM = 146° _____

8. m∠QRN when m∠MNR = 52° _____

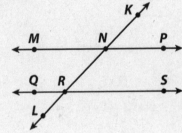

If m∠RNP = (8x + 63)° and m∠NRS = 5x°, find the following angle measures.

9. m∠RNP = _____

10. m∠NRS = _____

In the figure at the right, there are no parallel lines. Use the figure for problems 11–14.

11. Name both pairs of alternate exterior angles.

    _____

12. Name the corresponding angle to ∠4 _____

13. Name the relationship between ∠3 and ∠6.

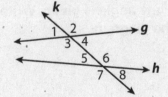

    _____

14. Are there any supplementary angles? If so, name two pairs. If not, explain why not.

    _____

**LESSON
21-1**

Parallel Lines Cut by a Transversal
Reteach

Parallel Lines	**Parallel Lines Cut by a Transversal**	
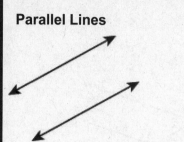 Parallel lines never meet.	A line that crosses parallel lines is a **transversal**. Eight angles are formed. If the transversal is not perpendicular to the parallel lines, then four angles are acute and four are obtuse. The acute angles are all congruent. The obtuse angles are all congruent. Any acute angle is supplementary to any obtuse angle.	120°/60° 60°/120° 120°/60° 60°/120°

In each diagram, parallel lines are cut by a transversal. Name the angles that are congruent to the indicated angle.

1.

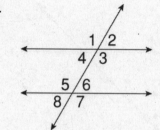

The angles congruent to

∠1 are: _____

2.

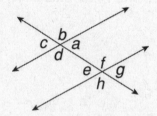

The angles congruent to

∠a are: _____

3.

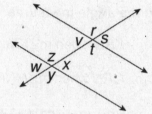

The angles congruent to

∠z are: _____

In each diagram, parallel lines are cut by a transversal and the measure of one angle is given. Write the measures of the remaining angles on the diagram.

4.

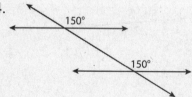

5.

6.

Name _____ Date _____ Class_____

Angle Theorems for Triangles
Practice and Problem Solving: A/B

Find the measure of each unknown angle.

1.

2.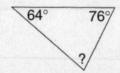

3.

_____   _____   _____

4.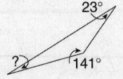

5.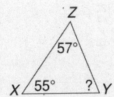

6.

_____   _____   _____

7.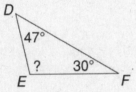

8.

9.

_____   _____   _____

Use the diagram at the right to answer each question below.

10. What is the measure of ∠*DEF*?

_____

11. What is the measure of ∠*DEG*?

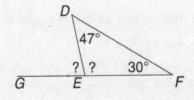

_____

12. A triangular sign has three angles that all have the same measure. What is the measure of each angle?

_____

LESSON
21-2

Angle Theorems for Triangles
Reteach

If you know the measure of two angles in a triangle, you can subtract
their sum from 180°. The difference is the measure of the third angle.

The two known angles are 60° and 55°.

$$60° + 55° = 115°$$

$$180° - 115° = 65°$$

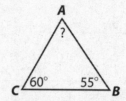

Solve.

1. Find the measure of the unknown angle.

   Add the two known angles: ____ + ____ = ____

   Subtract the sum from 180°: 180 – ____ = ____

   The measure of the unknown angle is: ____

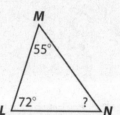

2. Find the measure of the unknown angle.

   Add the two known angles: ____ + ____ = ____

   Subtract the sum from 180°: 180 – ____ = ____

   The measure of the unknown angle is: ____

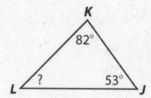

∠*DEG* is an **exterior angle**.

The measure of ∠*DEG* is equal to the sum of ∠D and ∠F.

$$47° + 30° = 77°$$

You can find the measure of ∠*DEF* by subtracting 77°
from 180°.

$$180° - 77° = 103°$$

The measure of ∠*DEF* is 103°.

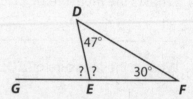

Solve.

3. Find the measure of angle *y*.

   $$85° + 65° = \text{_____}$$

4. Find the measure of angle *x*.

   $$180° - \text{____} = \text{____}$$

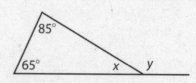

**LESSON
21-3**

Angle-Angle Similarity

Practice and Problem Solving: A/B

Explain whether the triangles are similar.

1.

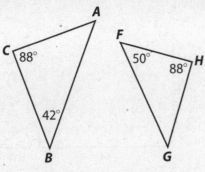

2.

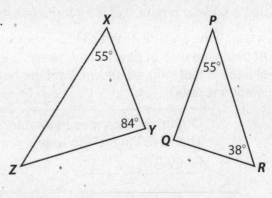

_____   _____

_____   _____

_____   _____

**The diagram below shows a Howe roof truss, which is used to frame
the roof of a building. Use it to answer problems 3–5.**

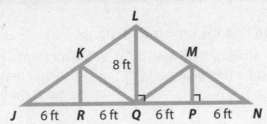

3. Explain why △*LQN* is similar to △*MPN*.

_____

4. What is the length of support *MP*? _____

5. Using the information in the diagram, can you determine whether
   △*LQJ* is similar to △*KRJ*? Explain.

_____

6. In the diagram at the right, sides *SV* and
   RW are parallel.
   Explain why △*RTW* is similar to △*STV*.

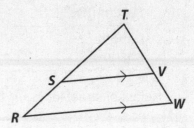

   _____

   _____

   _____

LESSON
21-3

Angle-Angle Similarity
Reteach

When solving triangle similarity problems involving proportions, you can use a table to organize given information and set up a proportion.

A telephone pole casts the shadow shown on the diagram. At the same time of day, Sandy, who is 5 feet tall, casts a shadow 8 feet long, as shown. Find the height of the telephone pole.

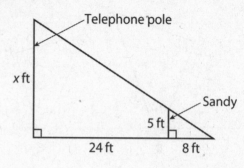

> **Organize distances in a table.** Then use the table to write a proportion.

	Pole	Sandy
Height (ft)	x	5
Length of shadow (ft)	24 + 8, or 32	8

$$\frac{x}{32} = \frac{5}{8}$$

Solve the proportion. The height of the telephone pole is 20 feet.

Complete the table. Then find the unknown distance.

1. A street lamp casts a shadow 31.5 feet long, while an 8-foot tall street sign casts a shadow 14 feet long.

2. A 5.5-foot woman casts a shadow that is 3 feet longer than her son's shadow. The son casts a shadow 13.5 feet long.

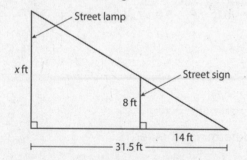

	Lamp	Sign
Height (ft)		
Length of shadow (ft)		

	Woman	Son
Height (ft)		
Length of shadow (ft)		

Height of street lamp = _____

Height of son = _____

LESSON 22-1

Volume of Cylinders
Practice and Problem Solving: A/B

Find the volume of each cylinder. Round your answer to the nearest tenth if necessary. Use 3.14 for π.

1. 6.5 cm

16 cm

_____

2. ⊢— 4 in. —⊣

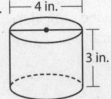

3 in.

_____

3. A cylindrical oil drum has a diameter of 2 feet and a height of 3 feet. What is the volume of the oil drum?

_____

4. New Oats cereal is packaged in a cardboard cylinder. The packaging is 10 inches tall with a diameter of 3 inches. What is the volume of the New Oats cereal package?

_____

5. A small plastic storage container is in the shape of a cylinder. It has a diameter of 7.6 centimeters and a height of 3 centimeters. What is the volume of the storage cylinder?

_____

6. A can of juice has a diameter of 6.6 centimeters and a height of 12.1 centimeters. What is the total volume of a six-pack of juice cans?

_____

7. Mr. Macady has an old cylindrical grain silo on his farm that stands 25 feet high with a diameter of 10 feet. Mr. Macady is planning to tear down the old silo and replace it with a new and bigger one. The new cylindrical silo will stand 30 feet high and have a diameter of 15 feet.

   a. What is the volume of the old silo? _____

   b. What is the volume of the new silo? _____

   c. How much greater is the volume of the new silo than the old silo?

   _____

Name _____ Date _____ Class_____

LESSON 22-1

Volume of Cylinders

Reteach

You can use your knowledge of how to find the area of a circle to find the volume of a cylinder.

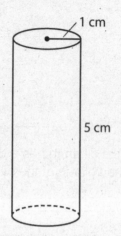

1. What is the shape of the base of the cylinder?

   _____**circle**_____

2. The area of the base is $B = \pi r^2$.

   $B = 3.14 \cdot \underline{\;1\;}^2 = \underline{\textbf{3.14}}$ cm²

3. The height of the cylinder is __**5**__ cm.

4. The volume of the cylinder is

   $V = B \cdot h = \underline{\textbf{3.14}} \cdot \underline{\;5\;} = \underline{\textbf{15.7}}$ cm³

The volume of the cylinder is 15.7 cm³.

---

1. a. What is the area of the base?

   $B = 3.14 \cdot \underline{\quad}^2 = \underline{\quad}$ cm²

   b. What is the height of the cylinder? _____ cm

   c. What is the volume of the cylinder?

   $V = B \cdot h = \underline{\quad} \cdot \underline{\quad} = \underline{\quad}$ cm³

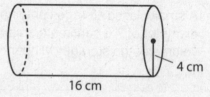

2. a. What is the area of the base?

   $B = 3.14 \cdot \underline{\quad}^2 = \underline{\quad}$ cm²

   b. What is the height of the cylinder? _____ cm

   c. What is the volume of the cylinder?

   $V = B \cdot h = \underline{\quad} \cdot \underline{\quad} = \underline{\quad}$ cm³

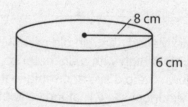

LESSON 22-2

Volume of Cones

Practice and Problem Solving: A/B

Find the volume of each cone. Round your answer to the nearest tenth if necessary. Use 3.14 for π.

1.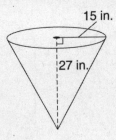

15 in.

27 in.

_____

2.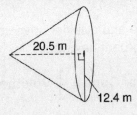

20.5 m

12.4 m

_____

3. The mold for a cone has a diameter of 4 inches and is 6 inches tall. What is the volume of the cone mold to the nearest tenth?

_____

4. A medium-sized paper cone has a diameter of 8 centimeters and a height of 10 centimeters. What is the volume of the cone?

_____

5. A funnel has a diameter of 9 in. and is 16 in. tall. A plug is put at the open end of the funnel. What is the volume of the cone to the nearest tenth?

_____

6. A party hat has a diameter of 10 cm and is 15 cm tall. What is the volume of the hat?

_____

7. Find the volume of the composite figure to the nearest tenth. Use 3.14 for π.

a. Volume of cone:

_____

b. Volume of cylinder:

_____

c. Volume of composite figure:

_____

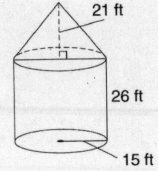

21 ft

26 ft

15 ft

LESSON
22-2
Volume of Cones
Reteach

You can use your knowledge of how to find the volume of a cylinder to help find the volume of a cone.

This cone and cylinder have congruent bases and congruent heights.

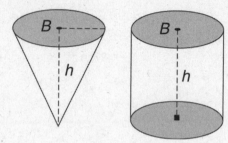

Volume of Cone $= \dfrac{1}{3}$ **Volume of Cylinder**

Use this formula to find the volume of a cone.

$$V = \dfrac{1}{3}Bh$$

Complete to find the volume of each cone.

1.

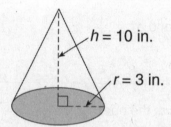

$h = 10$ in.

$r = 3$ in.

radius r of base = ____ in.

$V = \dfrac{1}{3}Bh$

$V = \dfrac{1}{3}(\pi r^2)h$

$V = \dfrac{1}{3}(\pi \times \text{\_\_\_}) \times \text{\_\_\_}$

$V = \dfrac{1}{3}(\text{\_\_\_}) \times \text{\_\_\_}$

$V = \text{\_\_\_} \times \text{\_\_\_}$

$V = \text{_____}$

$V \approx \text{\_\_\_}$ in^3

2.

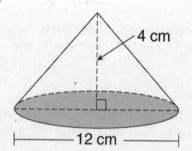

4 cm

12 cm

radius $r = \dfrac{1}{2}$ diameter = ____ cm

$V = \dfrac{1}{3}Bh$

$V = \dfrac{1}{3}(\pi r^2)h$

$V = \dfrac{1}{3}(\pi \times \text{\_\_\_}) \times \text{\_\_\_}$

$V = \dfrac{1}{3}(\text{\_\_\_}) \times \text{\_\_\_}$

$V = \text{\_\_\_} \times \text{\_\_\_}$

$V = \text{_____}$

$V \approx \text{\_\_\_}$ cm^3

Name _____ Date _____ Class_____

LESSON 22-3

Volume of Spheres

Practice and Problem Solving: A/B

Find the volume of each sphere. Round your answer to the nearest tenth if necessary. $V = \frac{4}{3}\pi r^3$. Use 3.14 for π. Show your work.

1.

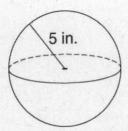

5 in.

_____

2.

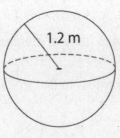

1.2 m

_____

3. $r = 3$ inches

_____

4. $d = 9$ feet

_____

5. $r = 1.5$ meters

_____

6. A globe is a map of Earth shaped as a sphere. What is the volume, to the nearest tenth, of a globe with a diameter of 16 inches?

_____

7. The maximum diameter of a bowling ball is 8.6 inches. What is the volume to the nearest tenth of a bowling ball with this diameter?

_____

8. According to the National Collegiate Athletic Association men's rules, a tennis ball must have a diameter of more than $2\frac{1}{2}$ inches and less than $2\frac{5}{8}$ inches.

   a. What is the volume of a sphere with a diameter of $2\frac{1}{2}$ inches?

   _____

   b. What is the volume of a sphere with a diameter of $2\frac{5}{8}$ inches?

   _____

   c. Write an inequality that expresses the range in the volume of acceptable tennis balls.

   _____

LESSON 22-3

Volume of Spheres
Reteach

- All points on a sphere are the same distance from its center.
- Any line drawn from the center of a sphere to its surface is a radius of the sphere.
- The radius is half the measure of the diameter.
- Use this formula to find the volume of a sphere.

$$V = \frac{4}{3}\pi r^3$$

Complete to find the volume of each sphere to the nearest tenth. Use 3.14 for π. The first one is done for you.

1. A regular tennis ball has a diameter of 2.5 inches.

   diameter = __2.5 inches__

   radius = __1.25 inches__

   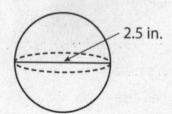

   2.5 in.

   $V = \frac{4}{3}\pi r^3$

   $V = \frac{4}{3} \cdot \underline{3.14} \cdot \underline{1.25^3}$

   $V = \frac{4}{3} \cdot \underline{3.14} \cdot \underline{1.95}$

   $V = \underline{8.164}$

   $V \approx \underline{8.2 \text{ in}^3}$

2. A large grapefruit has a diameter of 12 centimeters.

   diameter = _____

   radius = _____

   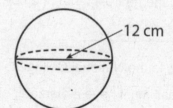

   12 cm

   $V = \frac{4}{3}\pi r^3$

   $V = \frac{4}{3} \cdot \underline{\hspace{1cm}} \cdot \underline{\hspace{1cm}}$

   $V = \frac{4}{3} \cdot \underline{\hspace{1cm}} \cdot \underline{\hspace{1cm}}$

   $V = \underline{\hspace{1cm}}$

   $V \approx \underline{\hspace{1cm}}$